A Hindu View of Arts

A Hindu View of Arts

Why Sanskar Bharati?

Dattopant Thengadi

PRABHAT
PAPERBACKS

Published by
PRABHAT PAPERBACKS
An imprint of Prabhat Prakashan Pvt. Ltd.
4/19 Asaf Ali Road,
New Delhi-110002 (INDIA)
e-mail: prabhatbooks@gmail.com

ISBN 978-93-90378-25-8
A HINDU VIEW OF ARTS
by Shri Dattopant Thengadi

Edition
2022

Price
₹ 150.00 (Rupees One Hundred Fifty only)

Printed at
R-Tech Offset Printers, Delhi

Publisher's Note

The twin objectives of Sanskar Bharati are: to promote the creativity, social appeal and educational quality of arts; and to realise in man the fulfilment of Satyam, Sivam, Sundaram. Art inspires and elevates. It lends dynamism to the compassion that is enshrined in the human heart. Art, compassion and humaneness form the one sacred confluence of our social life. It is to re-affirm this eternal principle and to re-establish every Fine Art in its pristine glory that Sanskar Bharati has been conceived. Mananeeya Dattopantji Thengadi has blessed Sanskar Bharati with this book, a tour-de-force which embodies a seer-vision of the lofty panorama of the world of Art. Gathering in its sweep the concepts of Art in the east and the west in different religious traditions of the world and in different climes and ages—this treatise is a classic to be studied and assimilated, to be cherished as a treasure of profound wisdom and insight, of scholarship and masterly exposition.

We are extremely grateful to him for giving us a comprehensive philosophy for our organisation and an inspiring motivation for our mission in the form of this book.

Contents

Part-I

INCOMPREHENSIBLE

PROGRESSIVE UNFOLDMENT

Netaji Subash Chandra Bose once wrote:

"In this mortal world, everything perishes and will perish, but the ideas, ideals and dreams do not."

On the Vijayadashami day of 1925, a Rishi had a vision.

A long-range vision of his motherland at the pinnacle of glory.

The formation of 'Sanskar Bharati' is an important stage in the process of progressive unfoldment of his vision.

A memorable milestone!

SANSKAR BHARATI

When was 'Sanskar Bharati' launched?

Formally, on January 1, 1981. But, informally, its spirit had started functioning in 1954.

Dr. K.D. Swaminathan informs us that despite a flood of publications in the western world about the Stone Age paintings of France, Spain, the Sahara, Northern Europe, Siberia, South Africa, Australia, and North, Central and South America, there has been no reference published outside India to its Stone Age paintings, until Bridget and Raymond Alehin in 1968 included a chapter on this in their

'Birth of Indian Civilisation'. All of the western general works on worldwide Stone Age Paintings pass over India with no more than half an inaccurate sentence in the entire mass of commentary.

In the sand-stone of Central India, there is a vast store of rock-painting covering a time-span of 8,000 years. In numbers, in variety of subject and style, and in scientific significance, no other area on the earth excels Deccan as a repository of Stone Age art.

In the sand-stone of Central India, there is a vast store of rock-painting covering a time-span of 8,000 years. In numbers, in variety of subject and style, and in scientific significance, no other area on the earth excels Deccan as a repository of Stone Age art.

Still, though the Archaeological Survey of India was established in 1861, and the first notice of the rock-painting in an archaeological context occurs in 1880, no serious effort to place the rock-paintings in a broad perspective was made before 1958, but the work then was in a very primitive stage.

In 1954, Vishnu Wakankar, of Vikram University, Ujjain, started a one-man campaign to let the world know about Indian painted pre-historic record. Since then, he has found and described hundreds of painted shelters in a triangular area with its base line extending from Varanasi to Udaipur in the north and its apex in Mysore in the south.

The recognition his work received on national and international planes is a recent history.

The Spirit of 'Sanskar Bharati' became alive and active on the first day of Wakankar's one-man campaign.

It acquired flesh and blood with the formal inauguration of the organisation at Lucknow.

The dreams of all such patriotic pioneers are materialised since they are blessed by the Rashtra-Shakti of Bharat.

'SANSKAR'

The term 'Sanskar' is frequently used but rarely under-stood. A common man considers 'Sanskar' as synonymous with education. Education, an activity highly noble in itself, is qualitatively different from Sanskar. Education is related to intelligence and Sanskar to mind, heart, soul. A highly educated person may be devoid of 'Sanskar', a highly 'Susamskrit' person may be least educated. 'Sanskar' is the cumulative effect of a number of factors—internal as well as external, subjective as well as objective. Art is one of the foremost among such factors. 'Sanskar Bharati' seeks to serve the cause of 'Sanskar' through the instrumentality of Art,—the Hindu Art.

Education, an activity highly noble in itself, is qualitatively different from Sanskar. Education is related to intelligence and Sanskar to mind, heart, soul. A highly educated person may be devoid of 'Sanskar', a highly 'Susamskrit' person may be least educated.

HINDU ART AND HINDU MIND

Our country became independent before four decades. But the modern educated Hindu mind continues to be as slavish as before. An Anglicised Hindu will try to gauge every Indian situation by European' yardstick, understand every Indian problem from the European viewpoint, and look at everything Indian through European eyes. Nothing 'Hindu' can be considered to be great unless it is certified to be so by some western authority. Vivekananda became great—only after his Chicago Address. Ravindra—Sangeet was not a scientific form of music before Gurudeva was awarded the Nobel Prize. No piece of Hindu literature can be beautiful until it is appreciated by Schopenhauvers of European countries. For an Anglicised Hindu, 'a thing of beauty' does not automatically become 'a joy for ever'.

As compared to a typical, fashionable Hindu, a genuine virtuoso from the West can appreciate the Hindu Art more easily and in a better way. The Hindu Art cannot aspire to reach a modern Hindu heart except through the medium of some western testimonial.

As compared to a typical, fashionable Hindu, a genuine virtuoso from the West can appreciate the Hindu Art more easily and in a better way. The Hindu Art cannot aspire to reach a modern Hindu heart except through the medium of some western testimonial.

It is true that till recent times, there had been no earnest effort on the part of the Europeans to understand the heart of Hindustan.

In 'The Story of Civilisation, Vol.1: Our Oriental Heritage', Will Durant observes:

"Nothing should more deeply shame the modern student than the recency and inadequacy of his acquaintance with India. Here is a vast peninsula of nearly two million square miles, two-thirds as large as the United States, and twenty times the size of its master, Great Britain; 320,000,000 souls—more than in all North and South America combined, or one-fifth of the population of the earth; an impressive continuity of development and civilisation from Mohanjo-daro, 2900 B.C. or earlier, to Gandhi, Raman and Tagore; faiths compassing every stage from barbarous idolatry to the most subtle and spiritual pantheism; philosophers playing a thousand variations on one monistic theme from the Upanishads, eight centuries before Christ, to Sankara, eight centuries after him; scientists developing astronomy three thousand years ago, and winning Nobel prizes in our own time; a democratic Constitution of untraceable antiquity in the villages, and wise and beneficent rulers like Ashoka and Akbar in the capitals; minstrels singing great epics almost as old as Homer, and poets holding world audiences today;

Nothing should more deeply shame the modern student than the recency and inadequacy of his acquaintance with India. Here is a vast peninsula of nearly two million square miles, two-thirds as large as the United States, and twenty times the size of its master...

artists raising gigantic temples for Hindu Gods from Tibet to Ceylon and from Cambodia to Java, or carving perfect palaces by the score for Moghul kings and queens—this is the India that patient scholarship is now opening up, like a new intellectual continent, to that western mind which only yesterday thought civilisation an exclusively European thing."

HINDU ART AND WESTERNERS

In the distant past, Europeans must have had a very vague and faint impression about the nature of Hindu Art. In the last quarter of the eighteenth century, Francis Fowkes and Sir William Jones introduced the Vina of the Hindus and their Musical Modes to the West. The curiosity and interest of European art-lovers in the aesthetic aspect of Hindu life continued uninterruptedly. That gave rise on the one hand to ever-increasing appreciation by the genuine devotees of arts and, on the other, jealousy and anxiety on the part of imperialists and their stooges in the field of art. Consequently, we come across expressions of very high admiration and reprehensible vilification simultaneously.

In the distant past, Europeans must have had a very vague and faint impression about the nature of Hindu Art. In the last quarter of the eighteenth century, Francis Fowkes and Sir William Jones introduced the Vina of the Hindus and their Musical Modes to the West.

FOREIGN VIRTUOSITY

After coming in contact with Hindu Art, many art lovers of the West fell in love with it. They had genuine virtuosity. Their minds were not vitiated or polluted by extraneous considerations of political and economic imperialism. Here are a few exclamations:

Fergusson described the Jain temples of Vimala and Tejahpala on Mount Abu as "finished with a delicacy of detail and appropriateness of ornament which is probably unsurpassed by any similar example to be found anywhere else. Those introduced by the Gothic architects in Henry VII's Chapel at Westminster or at Oxford, are coarse and clumsy in comparison."

Edmund Gilles: "It is, in fact, the loss of meaning in the theatre of the Western world that had impressed us most, when we came away from this demonstration of 'Kathakali' and it seemed as if there were no limits to what we have yet to learn from the Eastern Theatre."

Edmund Gilles: "It is, in fact, the loss of meaning in the theatre of the Western world that had impressed us most, when we came away from this demonstration of 'Kathakali' and it seemed as if there were no limits to what we have yet to learn from the Eastern Theatre."

Goethe, who seems to have taken from Kalidasa the idea of prologue for his 'Faust', on 'Shakuntalam':

"Wouldst thou the young year's blossoms, and the fruits of its decline, and all by which the soul is charmed, enraptured, feasted, fed; wouldst thou the Earth and Heaven itself in sole name combine? I name thee, O Shakuntala! and all at once is said."

This should suffice.

FOREIGN CRITICS

But such virtuosity was exceptional.

Till recently, there was no proper appreciation of Hindu Art in the West. It was much misunderstood, misrepresented and maligned. Often, there were torrents of sweeping denunciations by deliberately hostile critics. The Ajanta School was 'a local development of the cosmopolitan art of the contemporary Roman Empire' and the painting in Cave I was 'a vivid representation of the ceremonial attending the presentation of their credentials by the Persian envoys', which is a signal proof of the derivative character of the Ajanta School. "There are wide gaps in the history of your Hindu painting. It has not produced any Michael Angelo, Titian or Tintoretto. It is also inferior to modern paintings marked by abstractness or surrealism, influenced by the 'OP Art' and the 'Kinetic Art', and trying to evolve the modern technique of 'Futurism'. 'The artistic Indian temples cannot be compared with Greek

Till recently, there was no proper appreciation of Hindu Art in the West. It was much misunderstood, misrepresented and maligned. Often, there were torrents of sweeping denunciations by deliberately hostile critics.

Parthenon or Italian Church or Duomo or Campanile or the Gothic Cathedrals of medieval France. Hindu artists were ignorant of the Hellenised conception of rational beauty. In the Indian architecture, there is no trace of unity, clarity or classic nobility. Everything is ponderous, everything overwrought, devoid of lightness and lucid grace. The whole thing is a monstrosity built by demons, ogress—a gigantesque barbarism. The dance of Shiva is a dance of Death or Destruction,—an unrestrained outburst of the primitive, tribal vital energy. Indian theatre offers no scope for creativity and imagination. Hindu sculpture is inferior to its European counterpart—to Hellenic sculpture. It is absurd, captious, exaggerated, uncouth, strange, bizarre—the work of a distorted imagination labouring mid a nightmare of unlovely realities and devoid of naturalism.'

Indian theatre offers no scope for creativity and imagination. Hindu sculpture is inferior to its European counterpart—to Hellenic sculpture. It is absurd, captious, exaggerated, uncouth, strange, bizarre—the work of a distorted imagination labouring mid a nightmare of unlovely realities and devoid of naturalism.'

SYMPATHETIC MINDS

One may not worry about the uncharitable remarks by those who are thoroughly prejudiced against us and intentionally bent upon devaluing everything Hindu. But what about such westerners who are not unsympathetic? They realise that there is a difference between Indian traditional principles and western traditional principles of Art, and that a good critic should judge any piece of art by doing research on the artist's environment, his touch with history, the change in the artist's mind created by the visuals and also by his individual character. The reason lies in the fact that they are not generally conversant with the characteristic Hindu Mind.

INTEGRAL APPROACH

> ***Hindus are known for their integrated thinking and inter-disciplinary approach. They are aware that Art cannot be considered in isolation. Art is part and parcel of general life and culture. Even Science and Art cannot be completely compartmentalised.***

Hindus are known for their integrated thinking and inter-disciplinary approach. They are aware that Art cannot be considered in isolation. Art is part and parcel of general life and culture. Even Science and Art cannot be completely compartmentalised. At a certain stage, development of science becomes an art, even as at a certain stage, development of art becomes a science. The material and the spiritual also cannot be completely compartmentalised. Einstein was of the view that science without religion is lame, religion without science is blind. At its highest stage of development, science becomes one with spiritualism. As Dr. Fritzof Capra says,

"The basic oneness of the universe is not only the central characteristic of the mystical experience, but is also one of the most important revelations of modern physics." Tolstoy concludes: "The highest wisdom has but one science, the science of the whole, the science explaining the whole creation and man's place in it." Sanatana Dharma, of which the latest manifestation is Deendayalji's Ekatma Manava Darshan, has the realisation of this fact as one of its basic tenets. Art is also to be considered as an integral part of the whole.

The aims and objects of 'Sanskar Bharati', an all-India organisation dedicated to the cause of fine arts are to be viewed, studied, and evaluated against this background.

Art has no parallel. It inspires and elevates. In its pursuit, the Artist enjoys supreme bliss, and the audience is literally entranced. It wipes off the sorrow of the afflicted and infuses enthusiasm in the disheartened and the disappointed. It lends dynamism to the compassion that is enshrined in the human heart.

"Art has no parallel. It inspires and elevates. In its pursuit, the Artist enjoys supreme bliss, and the audience is literally entranced. It wipes off the sorrow of the afflicted and infuses enthusiasm in the disheartened and the disappointed. It lends dynamism to the compassion that is enshrined in the human heart.

Compassion and sensitivity propel man to progress and act as divine nector for humanity. In fact, family, society and humanity are merely the expressions of this one quality, compassion. In its absence, man loses his humanness and society its very existence. Art, compassion and humanness form the one sacred confluence of our social life.

Compassion and sensitivity render man susceptible to Sanskar. Through Sanskar lies the path of nature's pilgrimage to culture. Human history bears testimony to this."

'Sanskar Bharati' rightly considers fine arts as a divine gift to humanity pursuing its eternal quest after emancipation. Fine arts help the man develop refinement and enlightenment in him, through the medium of sweet, beautiful, rejuvenative and captivating entertainment. This is one of the important vehicles of 'Sanskar'.

'Sanskar Bharati' rightly considers fine arts as a divine gift to humanity pursuing its eternal quest after emancipation. Fine arts help the man develop refinement and enlightenment in him, through the medium of sweet, beautiful, rejuvenative and captivating entertainment. This is one of the important vehicles of 'Sanskar'.

Primitive art had its origin in primitive sense of beauty. It continued to progress with the passage of time—the painting of the body, cosmetics, tatooing, sacrification, weaving, clothing, ornaments, pottery, general painting, magic, folklores and folksongs, parables, legends, allegories, mythologies, drawing, writing, script, language, primitive literature with its various forms, handicrafts, sculpture, architecture, song and dance, mimicry, music and drama, games and festivities.

With the advances in scientific knowledge, new dimensions were added to ancient arts and new arts were introduced. This was the case with every human activity. In his search for food, man moved from hunting, fishing, herding and domestication of animal, through agriculture, discovery of fire, and simple roasting, to the sophisticated cooking in the micro wave oven.

With the advances in scientific knowledge, new dimensions were added to ancient arts and new arts were introduced. This was the case with every human activity. In his search for food, man moved from hunting, fishing, herding and domestication of animal, through agriculture, discovery of fire, and simple roasting, to the sophisticated cooking in the micro wave oven.

He has moved from caves to skyscrapers, from barks to polyester, from primitive free love to romances of Marilyn Monroe. Science had naturally similar impact on the field of arts also.

But, inspite of this fact, it would be wrong to think of Art in isolation, as if it were an 'island'—a world in itself and by itself. The objects and events and factors leaving Sanskaras on human mind are innumerable. Sanskaras influence, and are influenced by, everything in the external and the internal world. Every ripple on human mind and every play of nature contribute to the moulding of Sanskaras. As Vivekananda remarked, "The truth gathered from internal experience is psychology, metaphysics and religion; from external experience the physical sciences. Now a perfect truth should be in harmony with experience in both the worlds." Sanskaras through arts constitute a pursuit of harmony at higher and still higher levels. The present state of our Sanskaras is a cumulative effect of every such thing in the past and the present. For correct, comprehensive and realistic appreciation of Sanskaras and arts, all these factors must be taken into account. In the absence of such an exercise, the view taken would be lopsided and imperfect.

Geological and geographical conditions; geopolitical factors; climates, weathers, natural resources, natural upheavals and vagaries of nature, floods, droughts, cyclones, famines, earthquakes, season-cycles, continental drifts, deluges, glaciation, volcanoes, geological cataclysms, epidemics, and environmental factors.

THE FACTORS

For example:

Geological and geographical conditions; geopolitical factors; climates, weathers, natural resources, natural upheavals and vagaries of nature, floods, droughts, cyclones, famines, earthquakes, season-cycles, continental drifts, deluges, glaciation, volcanoes, geological cataclysms, epidemics, and environmental factors.

Tools of production and destruction—from primitive tools to modern technology, and from sticks and stones to nuclear weapons,—and the impact of periodical changes in their nature and levels on individual, social and human psychology and inter-relationships.

Patterns of production, distribution, exchange, consumption and commercial intercourse.

Concepts about life, death, life after death, soul, God, the supernatural, religion, morals, metaphysics, virtue and vice, right and wrong, merit and sin, social regulations, customs, manners, etiquettes, costumes, festivals and ceremonials, and an ideal of a gentleman.

Objects of fear, wonder, dreams, contempt, admiration, respect and worship.

Attitude towards leisure, comforts and luxuries, stresses and strains, challenges and opportunities.

Popular belief-systems, superstitions, faith, instincts, sentiments, feelings, emotions, intuitions.

Conventional response to the sense of beauty, lust, sensuality, sexual anarchism, marriage institution with its various forms, pre-marital relations, prostitution, adultery, chastity, virginity, hypocricy in sexual matters, restraint, divorce, abortion, and infanticide.

Conventional response to the sense of beauty, lust, sensuality, sexual anarchism, marriage institution with its various forms, pre-marital relations, prostitution, adultery, chastity, virginity, hypocricy in sexual matters, restraint, divorce, abortion, and infanticide.

The impact of historical events, historical personalities, historical literature, changing world situations and frequent cultural intercourses.

The state of civilisation,—including social composition, economic and political institutional framework, moral value-system, quantum of knowledge, cultural level, popular thought-systems and recognised concepts about Time, Space and Cosmos.

A common man in the west may not discern it, but integrated thinking would reveal how all such factors influence, and are influenced, in varying degrees, by the nature, the development or the decline of Art.

□

Part II

THE APPROACH

GEOGRAPHICAL CONDITIONS

In 'Character and Climate', Huntington beautifully elaborates how climatic and geographical conditions affect the character of the people. He states, for example, that dry and cold climate of comparatively barren hilly areas would promote sturdy habits, while warm humidity of fertile plains would make people less industrious and more comfort-loving. The impact of mediterranean climate would be qualitatively different from that of the Northern climate. Climatic conditions have something to do with the fact of people being broadly extrovert or introvert. Recently, a columnist has humourously stated that though in the western love affair, a lover may use a Shakespearean expression to woo his beloved and say: "Shall I compare thee to a summer's day?" in the Indian environment, the same words may give a different impression, convey a different mental association to the beloved. It would mean that the romantic lover is seeking permission to compare his true love to unbearable heat, excessive humidity, shortage of water, sweat-stained clothes, dehydration, frayed tempers, sweaty under-arms, misty glasses, dry throats—to mention a few images that jump to mind.

Is it not understandable that members of nomadic tribes in the agriculturally undeveloped desert areas cannot afford to be individualistic? Their very survival demands that they should be collectivistic, mobile, disciplined, owing full allegiance to one leader. Members of settled agricultural communities are not compelled to cultivate these traits. Their mode of production is conducive to the growth of individualism and decline in social solidarity,—which is to be compensated by strong cultural activities.

Large areas of Eurasia have been victims of frequent barbaric invasions. The cockpits of constantly warring groups cannot be expected to be the centres of systematic growth of arts and culture, of intellectual and spiritual pursuits.

Large areas of Eurasia have been victims of frequent barbaric invasions. The cockpits of constantly warring groups cannot be expected to be the centres of systematic growth of arts and culture, of intellectual and spiritual pursuits.

The general psychology of Italians is bound to be different from that of Germans whose homeland is a 'camp in the open field'.

Israel and Switzerland cannot have the same psychology. The peculiar, isolated, geographical position of Britain contributed substantially to its attempt to become a major naval power ruling the waves.

Has not geography helped Russia whose vast hinterland and 'Marshal Winter' defeated Napolean and obstructed Hitler's armies?

Can one conceive of the people of the United States conducting their uninterrupted march towards material prosperity had the Almighty placed their country in the unfortunate geographical position of Poland? A part of their present abundance they owe to the intervening Atlantic.

Can one conceive of the people of the United States conducting their uninterrupted march towards material prosperity had the Almighty placed their country in the unfortunate geographical position of Poland? A part of their present abundance they owe to the intervening Atlantic.

Geopolitics was not completely wrong when it predicted in the first decade of this century that Britain would continue to enjoy its central position until some or any pails of the globe remained unexplored, and that once the world became a closed system, no longer in need of further explorations, that tiny island would lose its glorious position, and the world-centre would shift first to the 'Home Island' comprising Africa and Eurasia, and next to the hinterland of that 'Home Island' which extended from the Himalayas to the Arctic region.

The geographical position of Bharat in Asia is similar in many respects to that of Italy in Europe.

GEOGRAPHY AND ART

The relationship between Geography and Art has gone almost unnoticed in our country. An article by Sister Violita

A.C. in "Recent Trends and Concepts in Geography" explains how geography has influenced Indian music.

The music of India differs from place to place, but we can distinguish two broad divisions—the Northern Hindustani music and the Southern Carnatic music. The North had to face many invasions and consequently produced fighting races. The south had a more peaceful existence and people there had time to cultivate and become farmers. They had not many opportunities to mix with foreigners and so remained conservative and isolated. This is reflected in their music, which has remained conservative and classical.

The music of India differs from place to place, but we can distinguish two broad divisions—the Northern Hindustani music and the Southern Carnatic music. The North had to face many invasions and consequently produced fighting races.

Nature plays a very important part in the music of India. India has different music for different seasons and different parts of the day as also for elements of nature. Certain 'ragas' project the image of spring. 'Raga Malhar' brings to mind the distant echoes of the sound of thunder and the pitter patter of rain drops. It brings the odour of the earth and of green vegetation, the cry of the peacock and the call of the koel. Several 'ragas' have evolved in tune with the monsoon season, which give one the feeling of gathering clouds and the downpour of rain. 'Raga Bhatiyali' reflects the steady flow of the rivers of Bengal and the fishermen singing in mournful strains as they plod homeward through the twilight.

The strains of ruggedness and the dryness of the rocks and sandy topography of the Marwar region are depicted in 'raga Mand'. The echoes of mountains and valleys and the flowing sound of water, as it rushes down the mountain slopes along with boulders and pebbles are amply heard in 'raga pahari'. 'Raga Bhairava', melancholy and sombre, is to be sung in the early morning when everything is quiet.

Early Punjabi folk music may be compared to a fast flowing mountain stream full of life and gladness. Later on, this folk-music also became the medium of telling tragic tales of legendary lovers and heroes which may be compared to a deep-flowing, steady river, majestic and slow like the Chenab itself which flows through the land of Punjab. Punjabi folk-music has some similarity to the music of certain West Asian countries. It is closer to these countries and was invaded by its people. The people of Punjab react strongly to joys and sorrows and this is reflected in their songs and music.

Early Punjabi folk music may be compared to a fast flowing mountain stream full of life and gladness. Later on, this folk-music also became the medium of telling tragic tales of legendary lovers and heroes which may be compared to a deep-flowing, steady river, majestic and slow like the Chenab itself which flows through the land of Punjab.

In Bihar, 'Sravan' being the monsoon season, one of hectic activity in the fields for men, they break into the songs known as 'Barsati'.

When one hears the Bengali folk-song, one can picture the typical rural life of the Bengalis as they perform their ordinary day-to-day work. The diversified nature of this music is due to the changing moods of life, to suit which the music is made. There is also a variation of music from district to district and to suit the variety of physical features of the land. There are songs descriptive of the wide fields and the rivers of Bengal, of seasons in their brightness and in their gloom, songs that express the hopes and dreams and frustrations of its people, their joys and sorrows, their harvests and festivals.

The speed of music varies with the environment. In warm climates, music is slower, more expansive and more intricate, whereas in colder climates, it is vigorous and loud.

The speed of music varies with the environment. In warm climates, music is slower, more expansive and more intricate, whereas in colder climates, it is vigorous and loud.

THOUGHT SYSTEMS

Religions, Ideologies, Thought Systems have their own role to play.

The term 'Thought System' is being deliberately used here.

The word 'Ideology' has been changing its connotation from to time. It is not being used today in the same sense in which it was first used during the Napoleonic period.

The word 'religion' has created more confusion than clarity. As Pt. Jawarharlal Nehru remarked, "No word perhaps in any language is more likely to be interpreted in different ways by different people as the word 'religion'... probably in no two persons will the same complex of ideas and images arise on hearing or reading this word. The word 'religion' has lost all precise significance (if it ever had) and only causes confusion and gives rise to interminable debate and argument, when often enough entirely different meanings are attached to it. It would be far better if it was dropped from use altogether and other words with more limited meanings were used instead, such as theology, philosophy, morals, ethics, spirituality, mataphysics, duty, ceremonial, etc."

No word perhaps in any language is more likely to be interpreted in different ways by different people as the word 'religion'... probably in no two persons will the same complex of ideas and images arise on hearing or reading this word.

No doubt, the term 'philosophy' had a specific meaning, that is, a pursuit of wisdom and knowledge; the science of being as being; the knowledge of the causes and laws of all things; the principles underlying any department of knowledge. But today it has become an over-worked coin,—losing precision and edge.

Hence, the propriety of introducing the term 'Thought Systems'.

Anyway, to illustrate our main point, we may conveniently skip over those that have become part of the past and have no successors in the present-day world.

JUDAISM

The fathers and founders of the Hebrew nation, Abraham, Isaac and Jacob had no time or facility for arts. They were followed by Moses. The 'Mosaic' code on which all later Jewish life was to be built elevated through its Second Commandment the national conception of God at the expense of art, no graven images were ever to be made of him. God must be beyond every form and image. The Commandment conscripted Hebrew devotion for religion, and left nothing, in ancient days, for science and art. Astronomy was neglected. In the new Temple, there was no imagery. The old images had been carried off to Babylon. We find no sculpture, painting or bas-relief after the Babylonian captivity. The priests allowed only some architecture and music.

The fathers and founders of the Hebrew nation, Abraham, Isaac and Jacob had no time or facility for arts. They were followed by Moses. The 'Mosaic' code on which all later Jewish life was to be built elevated through its Second Commandment the national conception of God at the expense of art, no graven images were ever to be made of him.

All the books that constitute the Old Testament were the sacred literature of the Jews, who, except for a small remnant of common people, had been deported to Babylonia from their own country in 587 B.C. by Nebuchadnezzar II, the Chaldean. They returned to their cities, Jerusalem, and rebuilt their Temple. King Soloman (960 B.C.) recast and revitalised the religion whose weak hold upon the racially and mentally confused Hebrews was creating problems. With the reign of King Soloman, the brief glory of the Hebrews ends. In course of time, this priestly temple religion became a prophetic religion. The Jews became gradually convinced that Jehovah was the only true god, that, as a people, they were the chosen people of the one God of all the earth, and that a Messiah would come to realise the Long-postponed promise of Jehovah. The concept of one 'Jealous' God who would have 'none other Gods', and the idea of a promise and of divine leadership gave to Judaism a quality (of intolerance) which no other contemporary religion could display. Buddhism, Confucianism, Lao-Tse-ism or Taoism had neither such rigidity, nor such vigour of intolerance.

The concept of one 'Jealous' God who would have 'none other Gods', and the idea of a promise and of divine leadership gave to Judaism a quality (of intolerance) which no other contemporary religion could display.

Out of this conviction arose the mental matrix of the Jews. It sustained them through their world-wide persecution of centuries. But though their genius, scattered all over the globe for centuries, contributed substantially to different cultures, their creativity could not be channelised during that long period for the cultural renaissance of their own homeland. The impact of the same, traditional mental matrix is discernable in their Herculian effort for national reconstruction and stiff resistance to the Arab world, after the birth of Israel. Presently, the need of the hour for Israel is the martial spirit of Sparta, and not the proverbial aesthetic sense of Florence.

ISLAM

Various terms connected to Mohamedanism are being used in a loose manner, creating confusion of thought. Particularly so in the field of arts—'Islamic Art', 'Moslem', 'Indo-Moslem', 'Moorish' or 'Indo-Saracenic' architecture, Mughal Art, Afghan style of architecture, Persian Art, etc.

No comprehensive effort to objectively assess the impact of Islam on various aspects of national and international life seems to have been made so far, though literature on Islam is flooding the world markets. There is no authentic book available on the topic of 'Secularism and Islam'. Treatises like the one by M.N. Roy are considered as exceptional. Various terms connected to Mohamedanism are being used in a loose manner, creating confusion of thought. Particularly so in the field of arts—'Islamic Art', 'Moslem', 'Indo-Moslem', 'Moorish' or 'Indo-Saracenic' architecture, Mughal Art, Afghan style of architecture, Persian Art, etc. Even in this field, politicians, who are ignorant of Arts, are playing havoc for their own partisan ends. It is being forgotten that every nation, people or tribe professing Islam as its religion has its own culture with its distinctive characteristics. M.N. Roy has this fact in his mind when he described invasions through Khyber as those by various tribes, such as Arabs, Mughals, etc., and not by Islam as such. The character of such invasions and of subsequent regimes differed, according to him, in keeping with the different characteristics of the invading tribes. Again, the unique architectural style of Persia or the Pyramids of Egypt were pre-Islamic. In our country, the Afghan dynasty used Hindu artisans, copied Hindu themes and even appropriated the pillars of Hindu temples for their architectural purposes, and many mosques were merely Hindu temples rebuilt for Moslem prayers. The architectural style at Fatehpur Sikri, Delhi and Agra is described as Mughal style. Today, the indigenous styles of music are being admirably practised and promoted by illustrious Muslim artists dedicated to music; and they are all respected as 'Sadhakas' of Deshi art. The case of Tansen was no different. Out of the seventeen artists (painters) considered prominent in Akbar's reign, thirteen were

The architectural style at Fatehpur Sikri, Delhi and Agra is described as Mughal style. Today, the indigenous styles of music are being admirably practised and promoted by illustrious Muslim artists dedicated to music; and they are all respected as 'Sadhakas' of Deshi art.

Hindus. No scholar of eminence has come forward to challenge the claims of P.N. Oke regarding Taj Mahal, Kutub Minar and other works. It is, however, recognised that Shah Jehan had utilised the talents of three foreign artists for designing Taj Mahal, an Italian, Gieronimo Veroneo; a Persian, Ustad Isa; and a Frenchman, Austin de Bordeaux (Lord William Bentick once thought of selling the Taj for $150,000 to a Hindu Contractor).

As a religion, Islam has influenced the character of people under its umbrella; but their native cultures have also had their impact on the local, and even general character of Islam. For a critical analysis of this entire phenomenon, another Roy will have to be born. But the fact remains that the temperament of Islam is not conducive to the growth of fine arts. Like Mosaic prohibition in Judea, the Islamic prohibition also obstructed the progress of arts in the Islamic world.

As a religion, Islam has influenced the character of people under its umbrella; but their native cultures have also had their impact on the local, and even general character of Islam. For a critical analysis of this entire phenomenon, another Roy will have to be born.

Recently, we had serials on Ramayana and Mahabharata on T.V. Can the life of Mohametd the Prophet, be serialised in the same manner? Whosoever undertakes this task will be required to invariably suggest or symbolise the presence of the 'Lord of the Desert' by the hind portion and tail of his camel, because the Holy Prophet cannot be shown on the screen. That would be against the tenets of Islam.

It is a recognised fact that the degree of Islam's influence on the minds of Aurangzeb and his predecessors was not the same. About Aurangzeb, Will Durant observes:

"Despite the screen, Aurangzeb was a misfortune for Mogul and Indian Art. Dedicated fanatically to an exclusive religion, he saw in art nothing but idolatry and vanity.... Indian art followed him to the grave."

"Despite the screen, Aurangzeb was a misfortune for Mogul and Indian Art. Dedicated fanatically to an exclusive religion, he saw in art nothing but idolatry and vanity.... Indian art followed him to the grave."

About the so-called 'Indo-Moslem Architecture' Sri Aurobindo comments: "I am not concerned to defend any claim for the purely indigenous origin of its features. It seems to me that here the Indian mind has taken in much from the Arab and Persian imagination and in certain mosques and tombs, I seem to find an impress of the robust and bold Afghan and Moghul temperament, but it remains clear enough that it is still on the whole a typically Indian creation with the peculiar Indian gift... whatever its beauty, it belongs entirely to a secondary plane of artistic creation and cannot rank with the great spiritual aspirations in stone of the Hindu builders." And, again, "There is not here indeed the vast spiritual content of the earlier Indian mind, but it is still an Indian mind which in these delicate creations absorbs the West Asian influence."

Concluding the chapter on Architecture, Will Durant remarks, "Hence, this little survey must conclude as it began, by confessing that none but a Hindu can quite appreciate the art of India, or write about it forgivably."

COMMUNISM

Communism, the latest Semitic religion, aspired, in keeping with its ideology, to evolve a new, 'proletarian culture'. The protagonists of 'proletarian culture' negated the national democratic traditions of the past and preached nihilism and formalism.

Communism, the latest Semitic religion, aspired, in keeping with its ideology, to evolve a new, 'proletarian culture'. The protagonists of 'proletarian culture' negated the national democratic traditions of the past and preached nihilism and formalism.

Lenin was partly in agreement with this line. He insisted .that all work "in the field of political education in general and in the field of art in particular should be imbued with the spirit of the class struggle...." Like all sciences, all arts also were expected to promote the cause of the Dictatorship. Lenin's programme stated that "the working people would be enabled to enjoy all art treasures created through the exploitation of their labour, but until then enjoyed exclusively by the exploiters." It was necessary to create a firm basis for the growth of the working people's powerful and inexhaustible creative potentialities."

Lenin considered socialist industrialisation, agricultural co-operation and cultural revolution as the three major inter-connected components of socialist construction. He did not perceive culture as something isolated, outside time and space. He saw it as being linked with all aspects of life. Cultural revolution contributed to political, economic and social development. To accomplish cultural revolution was more difficult than winning political power.

Lenin knew that to strengthen the political educational system of the communist state, it was necessaiy to acquire "the sum total of knowledge that the teachers have inherited from the bourgeoise'.

"Marxism", Lenin wrote, "has won its historic significance as the ideology of the revolutionary proletariat because, far from rejecting the most valuable achievements of the bourgeoise epoch, it has, on the contrary, assimilated and refashioned everything of value in more than two thousand years of the development of human thought and culture."

"Marxism", Lenin wrote, "has won its historic significance as the ideology of the revolutionary proletariat because, far from rejecting the most valuable achievements of the bourgeoise epoch, it has, on the contrary, assimilated and refashioned everything of value in more than two thousand years of the development of human thought and culture." And again, "We should make a deep-going and comprehensive analysis of it (i.e., the process of cultural transformation) just as of any other problem of socialist construction, with due account taken of the general laws governing the development of human society, local specific features of the country and each region." The pre-revolutionary cultural institutions could be put to use after a certain reorganisation in the course of the cultural revolution, which included, among other things, the tasks of transforming and developing the theatre, painting, musical culture and creating a new literature."

Along with the evolution of an integral socialist culture, the cultural revolution, Lenin thought, should carry further and facundate the best national features of each nationality.

For example, in the Central Asian Republic of Uzbekistan, there was an attempt to revive the suitable cultural traditions of its people, put them in touch with the achievements of literature, science and art, spanning many centuries, including the works of the outstanding mathematician and astronomer Mirzo Ulugbek, the encyclopaedic Sina, Muhammad Ibn-Musa Khorezmi, the great Uzbek poet and thinker Alisher Navoi and other luminaries who considerably advanced science and culture.

Along with the evolution of an integral socialist culture, the cultural revolution, Lenin thought, should carry further and facundate the best national features of each nationality.

However, the policy of Lenin was given a go-by by

his successor, though the Soviet Constitution of 1936 recorded the achievements of the country's successful industrialisation, collectivisation of agriculture and the cultural revolution in the first half of the thirties.

Stalin also strove for Russification of all national cultures within the U.S.S.R.

However, the policy of Lenin was given a go-by by his successor, though the Soviet Constitution of 1936 recorded the achievements of the country's successful industrialisation, collectivisation of agriculture and the cultural revolution in the first half of the thirties.

It implied the spread of the culture of the Russian people, the study of the Russian language-sweeping aside all special characteristics of different national cultures, dubbing them as obsolete and outdated, and regimentation of the educational system. The talented writers, poets, play wrights, artists, musicians, actors, as well as engineers, agronomists, doctors, teachers and scientists in all nationalities were subjected to the regimentation of Russification. The culture was no longer required to satisfy the evergrowing requirements of different categories of the population, encourage the independent artistic pursuits of the people, provide adequate opportunities for their special faculties and aesthetic tastes. Russian culture was imposed upon all non-Russian people in the imposing name of "world socialist culture".

It should, however, be noted that M. Gorbachev

initiated a revolutionary change in the entire thinking and policies of the Soviet state in this regard, when at the Joint Festive Meeting of the Central Committee of the CPSU, the Supreme Soviet of the U.S.S.R. and the RSFSR, on the 70th Anniversary of the October Revolution, he said: "Scholars, scientists, inventors, writers, journalists, artists, actors, and teachers—all those who work in various spheres of culture and education must be champions of Perestroika."

"An emperor knows how to govern when poets are free to make verses, people to act plays, historians to tell the truth, ministers to give advice, the poor to grumble at taxes, students to learn lessons aloud, workmen to praise their skill and seek work, people to speak of anything, and old men to find fault with everything."

It would not be impertinent to restate at this stage the Address of the Duke of Shao to King Li-Wang in 845 B.C.:

"An emperor knows how to govern when poets are free to make verses, people to act plays, historians to tell the truth, ministers to give advice, the poor to grumble at taxes, students to learn lessons aloud, workmen to praise their skill and seek work, people to speak of anything, and old men to find fault with everything."

'CHRISTIAN' OR 'EUROPEAN'

It is customary, though not rational, to treat European culture, European Art and European Science as synonymous with 'Christian' culture, 'Christian' Art and 'Christian'

Science. For a common man, there is no practical need to make any distinction between the two.

Jesus has been wielding tremendous influence on the mind of mankind. But that is not the case with Christianity. An average man is not aware that it would be unfair to bracket Christ with Christianity. Nevertheless, this is a basic point deserving the attention of every serious thinker.

Jesus has been wielding tremendous influence on the mind of mankind. But that is not the case with Christianity. An average man is not aware that it would be unfair to bracket Christ with Christianity. Nevertheless, this is a basic point deserving the attention of every serious thinker.

According to H.G. Wells, Jesus was the seed, rather than the founder of Christianity:

"It is necessary that we should recall the reader's attention to the profound differences between this fully developed Christianity of Nicaea and the teachings of Jesus of Nazareth. All Christians hold that the latter is completely contained in the former, but that is a question outside our province. What is clearly apparent is that the teaching of Jesus of Nazareth was a prophetic teaching of the new type that began with the Hebrew prophets. It was not priestly, it had no consecrated temple and no altar. It had no rites and ceremonies. Its sacrifice was 'a broken and a contrite heart'. Its only organisation was an organisation of preachers, and its chief function was the sermon. But the full fledged Christianity of the fourth century, though it preserved as its nucleus the teachings of Jesus in the Gospels, was mainly a priestly religion of a type already familiar to the world for thousands of years. The centre of its elaborate ritual was an altar, and the essential act of worship the sacrifice, by a consecrated priest, of the mass. And it had a rapidly developing organisation of deacons, priests, and bishops.... A very important thing for us to note is the role played by the Emperor in the fixation of Christianity. Not only was the Council of Nicaea assembled by Constantine the Great, but all the great councils, the two at Constantinople (381 and 553), Ephesus (431), and Chalcedon (451), were called together by the imperial power. And it is very manifest that in much of the history of Christianity at this time the spirit of Constantine the Great is as evident as, or more evident than, the spirit of Jesus."

The centre of its elaborate ritual was an altar, and the essential act of worship the sacrifice, by a consecrated priest, of the mass. And it had a rapidly developing organisation of deacons, priests, and bishops.... A very important thing for us to note is the role played by the Emperor in the fixation of Christianity.

Wells further says:

"Now it is a matter of fact that in the Gospels, all that body of theological assertions which constitute Christianity finds little support. There is no clear and emphatic assertion in these books of the doctrines which Christian teachers of all denominations find generally necessary to salvation. Except for one passage in St. John's Gospel, it is difficult to get any words actually ascribed to Jesus in which he claimed to be the Jewish Messiah.... and still more difficult is it to find any claim to be a part of the Godhead, or any passage in which he explained the doctrine of the Atonement or urged any scarifices or sacraments (that is to say, priestly offices) upon his followers. We shall see presently how later on all Christendom was torn by disputes about the Trinity. There is no evidence that the apostles of Jesus ever heard of the Trinity—at any rate from him. The observance of the Jewish Sabbath, again, transferred to the Mithraic Sunday, is an important feature of many Christian cults; but Jesus deliberately broke the Sabbath, and said that it was made for man and not man for the Sabbath. Nor did he say a word about the worship of his mother Mary, in the guise of Isis, the Queen of Heaven. All that is most characteristically Christian in worship and usage, he ignored. Sceptical writers have had the temerity to deny that Jesus can be called a Christian at all.... As

Except for one passage in St. John's Gospel, it is difficult to get any words actually ascribed to Jesus in which he claimed to be the Jewish Messiah.... and still more difficult is it to find any claim to be a part of the Godhead, or any passage in which he explained the doctrine of the Atonement or urged any scarifices or sacraments (that is to say, priestly offices) upon his followers.

remarkable is the enormous prominence given by Jesus to the teaching of what he called the Kingdom of Heaven, and its comparative insignificance in the procedure and teaching of most of the Christian Churches."

The doctrine of the Kingdom of Heaven, which was the main teaching of Jesus, plays so small a part in the Christian creeds. "Yet be it noted that while there was much in the real teachings of Jesus that a rich man or a priest or a trader or an imperial official or any ordinary respectable citizen could not accept without the most revolutionary changes in his way of living, yet there was nothing that a follower of the actual teaching of Goutama Sakya might not receive very readily, nothing to prevent a primitive Buddhist from being also a Nazarene, and nothing to prevent a personal disciple of Jesus from accepting all the recorded teachings of Buddha."

Soon after his baptism on April 25, 387 A.D., Augustine wrote a series of treatises on liberal arts, notably music. He drew up his own liberal arts syllabus. In a way, he gave recognition to the antique knowledge and the Roman system of education.

Originally, the Churchanity of St. Paul or the Pre-Augustine Christianity was not kind to fine arts.

Soon after his baptism on April 25, 387 A.D., Augustine wrote a series of treatises on liberal arts, notably music. He drew up his own liberal arts syllabus. In a way, he gave recognition to the antique knowledge and the Roman system of education.

Augustine condemned the pagan religion—he was a great critic of paganism—but unconsciously allowed elements of philosophy, rhetoric and antique learning, even aesthetics, to creep into his writings.

Victoria Ukolova observes: "And as a maker of the new Christian culture that would reign in Europe throughout the Middle Ages, he was eager to assimilate a definite portion of the heritage of Antiquity with the aim of securing a new intellectual and cultural synthesis.

"Augustine's multiplicity paved the way for a relatively flexible system of spiritual life in which the antique legacy served as a continual fount of learning, philosophical rationalism, and a sense of the poetic.

Augustine's multiplicity paved the way for a relatively flexible system of spiritual life in which the antique legacy served as a continual fount of learning, philosophical rationalism, and a sense of the poetic.

"The close attention that Augustine had paid to the antique culture.... would, in due course, serve as a sort of magnifying glass for the moving spirits of the Carolingian Renaissance, the philosophers and poets of the 12th century, which brought Antiquity closer to them. It was a fairly rough magnifying glass, to be sure, and would, at times, make things look bigger or smaller than life, and duller in texture. But that was not the main thing. For, as a result, the legacy of Antiquity became incorporated in the medieval culture and served as a link between generations that had by its none too simple and conflicting existence cleared the way for the true Renaissance."

The pagan trends continued in the arts of the early Middle ages. The entire medieval educational system was largely based on the same pillars as the late antique schools, duly adapted to fit the Christian intellectual environment. There was also a kind of assimilation of late antique traditions in literature.

The pagan trends continued in the arts of the early Middle ages. The entire medieval educational system was largely based on the same pillars as the late antique schools, duly adapted to fit the Christian intellectual environment. There was also a kind of assimilation of late antique traditions in literature.

Neoplatonsim of the 3rd and 4th centuries passed down to the medieval period ideas that did not always coincide with orthodox Christianity.

The search of an ascetic ideal was also initiated by Julian who was anti-Christian.

The Roman idea of universalist statehood retained its hold on the public mind. Charlemagne's empire, the Holy Roman Empire, the Slav Third Rome plan, and, finally, the endless theocratic pretensions of the papacy (Pope Gregory the Great) were inspired by this ideal of Roman statehood.

Even after Christianity became the State religion, the influence of Roman culture and Roman institutions continued. This period of transition and intertwinement lasted some centuries. The joyously emotional and artistic nature of the people's festivities and the brightness of pagan arts were in direct contrast to the tragic asceticism and religious fanaticism of humourless Christianity. People's interest in gladiators' fight, circus and other theatrical shows, horse races, shows of elephants and crocodiles, persisted.

The triumphant Church could not break Homer's Golden Chain that connected the Earth and the Heaven, the Antiquity and the Middle ages, the Antiquity and the Renaissance, the Antiquity and the newly born national cultures, and the antiquity and the present times.

The triumphant Church could not break Homer's Golden Chain that connected the Earth and the Heaven, the Antiquity and the Middle ages, the Antiquity and the Renaissance, the Antiquity and the newly born national cultures, and the antiquity and the present times.

Gregory introduced extensive use of music which reflected the singing of various nations, and the pagan rhythms.

Ambrose spurned ornate language and the intricacies of the late Roman rhetoric.

Christian writers borrowed many a miracle in the lives of saints from antique literature, and partly from barbarian mythology. Gregory was not an exception to this.

In course of time, Christianity had assimilated the antique paganism and the barbarian paganism. In his 'Moralia', even Gregory did not shrink from antique rhetoric, antique grammar/ and antique philosophy.

The pre-Christian luminaries continued to influence

the Christian world inspite of a revolt against them by Christian fathers like Pope Gregory famous for his 'Moralia' and 'Dialogues' (590-604), who asked: "What use can there be from grammarians, who corrupt us rather than show us the way? How can the sophistries of the philosophers Pythagorus, Socrates, Plato and Aristotle help us? What can we do with the songs of the impious poets—Homer, Virgil and Menander? What good, I ask you, are Sallust, Herodotus, Livy, and other pagan historians for the Christian family? Can the eloquence of Gracchus, Lysias, Demosthenis and Tullius rival the pure teaching of Christ? What use to us are the bizarre devices of Flaccus, Solinus, Varro, Plautus, and Cicero?"

Gregory, next in importance to Augustine, flourished in the late 6th and early 7th centuries. Though determined inwardly to crush paganism, Gregory allowed the use of ancient rites and customary celebrations. He retained intact the sanctity of the sanctuaries of the old gods of local and tribal population and introduced churches in them.

Though determined inwardly to crush paganism, Gregory allowed the use of ancient rites and customary celebrations. He retained intact the sanctity of the sanctuaries of the old gods of local and tribal population and introduced churches in them.

It was in Gregory's time that Rome turned from the once great imperial city into the Rome of St. Peter, with a claim to becoming the capital of the entire Christian world. (Seat of papacy was founded by Apostle Peter).

Obviously, Christianity had gone through the influence of pre-Christian Roman and barbaric paganism contact with Arabic culture in the thirteenth century, and the Renaissance. Plato, Artistotle, Homer, Virgil, Ovid, Ptolemy and Hippocrates, brought Europe on the threshold of the Renaissance, which gave rise to a new vision of the world, a new system of values and ideas, and a new artistic language.

THE RENAISSANCE

The most important period in European history before the Industrial Revolution has been that of the Renascence. The term means 're-birth' and is applied to the recovery of the entire western world. A part of the Renascence was a period of the 'Renaissance', an educational, literary and artistic revival that went on in Italy and the western world affected by Italy during the fourteenth, the fifteenth and the sixteenth centuries. The Renaissance was a revival due to the exhumation of classical art and learning; it was but one factor in the very much larger and more complicated resurrection of European capacity and vigour. (This period almost coincides with that of the Reformation which is characterised, more importantly, by Reformation within the church, of which St. Francis of Assisi was the precursor, and the foundation of the 'Society of Jesus' by Saint Ignatius of Loyola).

The most important period in European history before the Industrial Revolution has been that of the Renascence. The term means 're-birth' and is applied to the recovery of the entire western world.

This was a really multisplendoured period.

On the one hand, the Black Death of the fourteenth century; the peasants' wars of England, France and Germany, the upheavals of the labouring classes of western Eurupe; an illustrious line of religious rebels and martyrs of conscience; and, on the other, development of good paper in the fourteenth century, introduction of printing in the fifteenth century; the beginning of European literature with the replacement of local dialects by standard literary languages of different regions.

The heritage of pre-Christian Antiquity became the root and stem upon which were grafted the shoots of all the national cultures of Europe. Good keepers of these cultural treasures of Antiquity were the 'Last of the Romans' like Boethius, the last outstanding 6th century pagan philosopher.

The heritage of pre-Christian Antiquity became the root and stem upon which were grafted the shoots of all the national cultures of Europe. Good keepers of these cultural treasures of Antiquity were the 'Last of the Romans' like Boethius, the last outstanding 6th century pagan philosopher.

Springing up like flowers of a multitude of very distinctive and beautiful buildings, cathedrals, abbeys, Gothic town churches, town halls and fortifications, with strong towers and the emergence of Florence as the centre of the rediscovery, restoration and imitation of antique art—these were among the treasures.

During the period of Renaissance, western Europe

broke out into a galaxy of names that outshine the utmost scientific reputations of the best age of Greece. Leonardo da Vinci (1452-1519), Copernicus (1473-1543), Tyeho Brahe (1546-1601), Kepler (1571-1630), Gilbert (1540-1603), Galileo Galilei (1564-1642).

The 'Sadhakas' of fine arts were Leonardo de Vinci, Filippo Lippi, Botticelli, Donatello, Michaelangelo and Raphael.

This is the genesis of what is now termed as European culture, European science and European art, though, subsequently as a part of the western civilisation, Europe has advanced rapidly from Newtonian science through Industrial Revolution to the present post-Second-Industrial- Revolution period.

This is the genesis of what is now termed as European culture, European science and European art, though, subsequently as a part of the western civilisation, Europe has advanced rapidly from Newtonian science through Industrial Revolution to the present post-Second-Industrial-Revolution period.

NEW KNOWLEDGE

Every valuable addition to human knowledge naturally affects the thought systems that are rigid.

There was nothing in the original teachings of Jesus which would come in conflict with any newly discovered truths. But official Christianity adopted St. Paul's view expressed in his epistles and untraceable in the Gospels. Paul had no inclination to scrutinise the Aristotelian theories that had been popular during his period. Christianity built itself upon the theories of Paul, and not upon the injunctions of Jesus.

Galileo was made to recant his assertion that the earth moved round the sun, because any doubt that the world was not the centre of the universe seemed to strike fatally at the authority of Christianity.

The 'Origin of Species by Means of Natural Selection' and the 'Descent of Man' by Darwin gave a jolt to Christianity, its story of the first sin, and the reason for an atonement.

When Einstein established inter-convertibility of matter and energy, he had shaken the very foundations of Materialism which was based upon the Newtonian science. Consequently, the ideologies based upon Materialism lost their credibility in varying degrees.

When Einstein established inter-convertibility of matter and energy, he had shaken the very foundations of Materialism which was based upon the Newtonian science. Consequently, the ideologies based upon Materialism lost their credibility in varying degrees.

It is the considered opinion of the experts that modern technology, if not restrained by Technological Ombudsman, will not only change the modes of production and destruction, but, in fact, inaugurate an entirely new civilisation, and the human mind will not be able to keep pace with it.

In his editorial, welcoming the first landing of man on moon, G.T. Madkholkar had expressed an apprehension that further exploration and conquest of space by man, though highly commendable in itself, would cause a serious loss to the romantic literature and art in which moon and stars had the pride of place.

RENAISSANCE AND RENAISSANCE

It must be stressed here that the nature of Hindu Renaissance will be completely different from that of the European Renaissance.

James H. Cousins in his 'The Renaissance in India' put the question whether the word 'renaissance' at all applies since India has always been awake and stood in no need of reawakening.

It must be stressed here that the nature of Hindu Renaissance will be completely different from that of the European Renaissance. James H. Cousins in his 'The Renaissance in India' put the question whether the word 'renaissance' at all applies since India has always been awake and stood in no need of reawakening.

The word 'Renaissance' should be understood in the Bharatiya sense of it. True, 'the word carries the mind back to the turning-point of European culture to which it was first applied; that was not so much a reawakening as an overturn and reversal, a seizure of Christianised, Teutonised, fuedalised European by the old Graeco-Latin spirit and form with all the complex and momentous results which came from it. That is certainly not a type of renaissance that is at all possible in India.'

According to Aurobindo, it was spirituality which saved India always at every critical moment of her destiny, and it has been the starting point too of her renaissance. Any other nation under the same pressure would have long ago perished soul and body.

Sri Aurobindo says: "When the Renaissance of India is complete, she will have an awakening, not of the same brutal (i.e., German) kind, certainly, but startling enough, as to the real nature and capacity of the Indian spirit.

Aurobindo refers to the 'bitter effects of the great decline which came to a head in the eighteenth and nineteenth centuries', describes that period as 'the evening time from which, according to the Indian idea of the cycles, a new age has to start', and says that "It was that moment and the pressure of a superimposed European culture which followed it that made the reawakening necessary."

Sri Aurobindo says: "When the Renaissance of India is complete, she will have an awakening, not of the same brutal (i.e., German) kind, certainly, but startling enough, as to the real nature and capacity of the Indian spirit."

THE NATURE OF CULTURE

Without entering into the academic discussion about the connotation of the terms 'culture', 'civilisation' and 'Samskriti', and endorsing the view that 'culture', like 'Samskriti' should be presumed to be universal in character, one has to recognise the fact that in common parlance, the term 'culture' denotes a trend of impressions on the mind of a society which is peculiar to its own and which, again, is a cumulative effect of its passions, emotions, thought, speech and action throughout its history.

Consequently, every culture has its characteristic impact on every field of human activity. It has been rightly said that cultural differences arise from the manner in which social experience is analysed and articulated into concepts, symbols, values and attitudes. Culture is characteristic social self-consciousness. To cite one example: Not withstanding the fact that long before harmony was used in Western music, the hermitages of India echoed with Vedic hymns sung harmonically, it must be admitted that Indian music differs from Western music in that it has no place for harmony, while harmony forms an essential feature in Western music. Indian music is melodic in form expressing the natural language of emotion. Harmonisation gives depth to a melody decorating it and adding more charm to it. According to one expert, the reason for harmony in Western music and the lack of it in Indian music can be due to the very make-up of the people who live in these parts. The Indian finds it easier to unite himself with the infinite, rather that with his

Consequently, every culture has its characteristic impact on every field of human activity. It has been rightly said that cultural differences arise from the manner in which social experience is analysed and articulated into concepts, symbols, values and attitudes.

neighbour. The purpose of Indian music 'is to refine one's soul and discipline one's body, to make one sensitive to the infinite within one, to unite one's breath with the breath of space, one's vibrations with the vibrations of the cosmos'. Indians are usually concerned more about their family than about the outside groups. For all these reasons, the Indian musician is rather a soloist than a player making music with others as in the small groups of large orchestras of Western music. Being predominantly a soloist, skilful improvisation is one of the chief marks of the virtuoso.

The purpose of Indian music 'is to refine one's soul and discipline one's body, to make one sensitive to the infinite within one, to unite one's breath with the breath of space, one's vibrations with the vibrations of the cosmos'.

By contrast, the European's desire has been to form individuals into communities and he is ready in the process to forego his freedom. This is seen in his very life, be it in the sphere of worship, work, social life or music where orchestras are characteristic. In orchestras or chorales, each instrument or voice has its independence to a certain degree, but one has to bear in mind the presence of other voices and try to blend his voice or instruments with others in the group. In Indian music, the individuals in the group 'remain soloists never coalescing into a harmonic statement'. Orchestras, therefore, are contrary to Indian musical nature.

In 'Republic', Plato observed that 'a change in the style of music reflects a basic change in culture'.

In 'The Meaning and Process of Culture', Prof. G.C. Pande observes: "Indian social history has a very different rhythm, a very different tempo from that of Western history. In the West, social changes have been faster and, at times, revolutionary. The state has played a dominant role in the development of social life and the struggle for power has been sharper and more wide-ranging. Ideological commitments have been extreme and the tolerance of difference and opposition minimal. In its aspiration after rationality, Western thought has erected the incoherences of ethos and attitudes into irreconciliable contradictions demanding absolute choice. The Indian mind, on the other hand, has sought to govern social relations not by an abstract reason, but by intuition and compromise. It has met new challenges by modifying rather than rejecting older solutions.

In 'The Meaning and Process of Culture', Prof. G.C. Pande observes: "Indian social history has a very different rhythm, a very different tempo from that of Western history. In the West, social changes have been faster and, at times, revolutionary.

"Western humanism has emphasised man's power over nature and his fulfilment through it. Indian humanism has consisted in a tolerant philosophy of 'live and let live'. Instead of the conquest of Nature, it has upheld the ideal of adjustment to Nature at one level and that of emancipation from it at another. Instead of seeking freedom through power, it has sought freedom through self-control. In the west, religion has meant adherence to organised or institutionalised dogma and, thus, conformity to the group. In India, there has always been a very strong tradition emphasising the personal and trans-social nature of religion. The tradition of western society has been dominated by the pattern of city-life, the 'technical order of civilisation'. Western history is the history of Athens and Alexandria, Rome and Constantinople, Paris and London. It is a succession of well-marked transitions in social and political form, and, thus, permits easy periodisation. In the social and cultural traditions of India on the other hand, the older and the newer forms have continued side by side and this continuity stretches back to pre-historic times. Conservatism with the readiness to reinterpret the past has prevented revolutions, and the caste-system has damped the growth of class antagonisms and (class) conflicts. The history of Indian society is more easily divisible into overlapping phases that sharply divided periods; it presents the spectacle of an amazing continuity and heterogeneity within the ambit of overall progress and unity."

The history of Indian society is more easily divisible into overlapping phases that sharply divided periods; it presents the spectacle of an amazing continuity and heterogeneity within the ambit of overall progress and unity.

Rishi Aurobindo has put forth this point in a convincing manner. In the field of art, for example, he says:

"The Western mind is arrested and attracted by the

form, lingers on it and cannot get away from its charm; loves it for its own beauty, rests on the emotional, intellectual, aesthetic suggestions that arise directly from its most visible language, confines the soul in the body; it might almost be said that for this mind form creates the spirit, the spirit depends for its existence and for everything it has to say on the form. The Indian attitude to the matter is at the opposite pole to this view. For the Indian mind form does not exist except as a creation of the spirit and draws all its meaning and value from the spirit. Every line, arrangement of mass, colour, shape, posture, every physical suggestion, however many, crowded, opulent they may be, is first and last a suggestion, a hint, very often a symbol which is in its main function a support for a spiritual emotion, idea, image that again goes beyond itself to the less definable, but more powerfully sensible reality of the spirit which has excited those movements in the aesthetic mind and passed through them into significant shapes."

Compare crowded art galleries and overpictured walls there with our artistic things in secluded cave temples. An Indian temple is in its inmost reality an altar raised to the Divine Self, house of the Cosmic Spirit, an appeal and aspiration to the Infinite.

"Compare crowded art galleries and overpictured walls there with our artistic things in secluded cave temples. An Indian temple is in its inmost reality an altar raised to the Divine Self, house of the Cosmic Spirit, an appeal and aspiration to the Infinite."

"The sculpture of ancient and medieval India claims its place on the very highest levels of artistic achievement. We shall not find a sculptural art of a more profound intention, a greater spirit, a more consistent skill of achievement. An assured history of two millenniums of accomplished sculptural creation is a rare and significant fact in the life of a people. It is due to the close connection between the religious and philosophical and the aesthetic mind of the people. This is the greatness of Indian sculpture that it expresses in stone and bronze what the Greek aesthetic mind could not conceive or express and embodies it with a profound understanding of its right conditions and a native perfection."

In matter of art, the Western mind was long bound up as in a prison in the Greek and Renaissance tradition modified by a later mentality with only two side rooms of escape, the romantic and the realistic motives, but these were only wings of the same building.

"In matter of art, the Western mind was long bound up as in a prison in the Greek and Renaissance tradition modified by a later mentality with only two side rooms of escape, the romantic and the realistic motives, but these were only wings of the same building."

The world has witnessed the vandalism of iconoclasts, Moslems destroying non-Muslim art and architecture recklessly, the Portugese smashing statutory and bas-reliefs at Elephanta barborously, the armies of Allah burning the famous Library of Alexandria. In contrast, see the hundreds of Cave-temples built in the early centuries of our era for Jains, Vedicists and Buddhists. Temples of Jains, Vaishnavites and Shaivites coexisting amicably and honourably for centuries at Khajuraho. Under the culture of Crusaders, this would have been inconceivable.

Language is constantly subject to the process of change springing from changes in the style of culture. Languages change under the impact of cultural factors in accordance with their phonetic and structural plausibilities. No doubt, certain basic institutions and attitudes show relatively minor variation in the course of culture and new meanings are often built out of old ones. But in the area of semantic change, we enter a realm of almost unlimited possibilities since it runs parallel to general cultural change. Cultural change leads to variation in the frequency of different types of discourses and this affects the repeat rate of words in the lexicon or language. Consequently, words become obsolete, new words emerge, and a total redistribution takes place. This is a basic process of semantic change. Indo-European languages have changed far more than semitic languages, because of the much greater cultural changes which the Indo-European people have undergone.

Language is constantly subject to the process of change springing from changes in the style of culture. Languages change under the impact of cultural factors in accordance with their phonetic and structural plausibilities.

The same is the case with philosophy. Even 'humanism'

changes its character as it travels from the East to the West.

The Western humanism, Revered Sri Guruji used to say, is homocentric. This is not the case with Hindu humanism, which is derived from the realisation of the supreme truth that 'All is One'.

Nolini Kanta Gupta says, "Humanism proper was born or reborn with the Renaissance. It was as strongly and vehemently negative and protestant in its nature as it was positive and affirmative. For its fundamental character—that which gave its very name—was a protest against, a turning away from whatever concerned itself with the supra-human, with God or self, with heaven or other worlds, with abstract or transcendental realities. The movement was 'humanistic' precisely because it stood against the Theological and Theocratical mediaeval age."

The Western humanism, Revered Sri Guruji used to say, is homocentric. This is not the case with Hindu humanism, which is derived from the realisation of the supreme truth that 'All is One'.

Dr. Maistre laments,

"I have seen in my time. Frenchmen, Italians, and Russians, I even know, thanks to Mantesquieu, that one may be a Persian, but as for Man, I declare that I have never met him in my life; if he exists, it is without my knowledge."

"The path of modern culture leads from humanity, through nationality, to beastiality." Obviously, the reference to 'modern culture' here is in the sense of 'Western Culture'.

Fritjog Capra feels,

"The Westeners so far favoured rational knowledge over intuitive wisdom, science over religion, competition over co-operation, exploitation of natural resources over conservation, and these factors among others have led to a profound cultural imbalance which lies at the very root of our current crisis... an imbalance in our thoughts and feelings, our values and attitudes and our social and political structures. The current crisis is a transition from sensate culture. As individuals, as a society, as a civilisation and as a planetary eco-system, we are reaching the turning point. What we need then is a new paradigm.... a new vision of reality, a fundamental change in our thoughts, perceptions and values."

The current crisis is a transition from sensate culture. As individuals, as a society, as a civilisation and as a planetary eco-system, we are reaching the turning point. What we need then is a new paradigm.... a new vision of reality, a fundamental change in our thoughts, perceptions and values.

The pathetic effect of this 'cultural imbalance' on the western attitude towards 'culture' itself is horrible. An extremist viewpoint on this subject has been expressed by one Lawrence Lovel in 'At War with Academic Traditions in America':

"Nothing in the world is more elusive (than culture)— An attempt to encampass its meaning in words is like trying to seize the air in the hand, when one finds that it is everywhere except within one's grasp."

Culture moulds the values of life. Our culture has blessed us with different values of life. Pt. Jawaharlal Nehru remarked, "We in India have been conditioned throughout our history in a peculiar way. Our greatest leader of modern times was neither a man of wealth, nor of military power, nor of position, yet millions of Indians bowed their heads before him and tried to follow his great lead. This is the type of man we honour, and I hope this is the type of man we shall always honour, even in the modern world."

We in India have been conditioned throughout our history in a peculiar way. Our greatest leader of modern times was neither a man of wealth, nor of military power, nor of position, yet millions of Indians bowed their heads before him and tried to follow his great lead. This is the type of man we honour, and I hope this is the type of man we shall always honour, even in the modern world.

For a western mind, this is a miracle. How could this be achieved? P.H. Prabhu observes, "The one big difference between the origin, development and stability of social classes in India and anywhere else is that elsewhere class-status is acquired as a concomitant or corollary of wealth, and is accompanied by power and authority, whereas in Hindu India, a perfect dissociation was attempted, and even achieved, between wealth and status, between power and authority, between disinterested pursuit and achievements in science on the one hand, and temptations of worldly comforts, on the other."

HINDU AESTHESIS

Ours is a deductive culture. The culture in which the whole of the structure of human life is based upon the perfect relationship between man and cosmos is termed as 'deductive culture'. Any action of a person not in tune with the ultimate goal of life is considered to be out of tune with aesthetic sense also. The concept of 'beauty' that dominated the Greek mind was substantially different from its Hindu concept. The line and run and turn demanded by the Indian aesthetic sense are not the same as those demanded by the European. A Hindu may not fully appreciate the beauty of the pieces of Tintoretto, the muscular Adam and beautiful Eve, the St. George slaying the dragon, the Christ appearing to Venetian Senators. Freud's theory is acceptable to Hindus only to a very limited extent. A beautiful damsel is attractive; generally, this need not be considered as a controversial statement. But, then, a small child with an innocent smile is also beautiful, though it does not arouse in average mind the same passion that one experiences at the sight of the feminine beauty. The starry

Freud's theory is acceptable to Hindus only to a very limited extent. A beautiful damsel is attractive; generally, this need not be considered as a controversial statement. But, then, a small child with an innocent smile is also beautiful, though it does not arouse in average mind the same passion that one experiences at the sight of the feminine beauty.

nights, the Himalayan peaks, the confluence of the rivers or seas, the fresh dawns—all these objects of nature also arouse one's aesthetic sense, though they are not the messengers of Freudian libido. Nor is our instinct of possessiveness roused by their divine beauty. We simply appreciate and enjoy, forgetting our self-consciousness. To us, all these are not 'of the earth, earthy'. There is an unconscious realisation that the scenes are far away from the Earth and nearer the Heaven or by whatever other name one may describe it. What we experience is a pure, unalloyed joy making us oblivious of our petty selves. This mental state is a big step ahead even for a confirmed atheist in the direction of spiritual ecstacy which he may actually experience without knowing the true nature of his own experience. The Hindu aesthesis is a highway to the spiritual experience combining in itself the supreme Truth, the supreme Knowledge and the supreme Joy—the Sat-Chit-Ananda. 'Nasadeeya' has been the first-ever aesthetic expression of human mind. The thread of its spirit can be discerned throughout the literature and art of all these centuries. In masterpieces like 'Amritanubhava', it is impossible to draw a line of demarcation between aesthesis and spirituality. Tithonus, Omar Khayyam, Casanova represent one type of aesthesis; the Vedic sages, a Jnaneshwara, a Vivekananda and others represent the other,

There is an unconscious realisation that the scenes are far away from the Earth and nearer the Heaven or by whatever other name one may describe it. What we experience is a pure, unalloyed joy making us oblivious of our petty selves.

and a higher level of virtuosity. Both culminate in joy. But in one case, the joy is immediate and finite, while in the other, it is eternal and infinite. The perfectibilian Hindu aesthesis blossoms into spiritualism. In no other culture this stage is reached.

The indispensability of spiritualism has been spelt out by Pandit Nehru in the following words:

"In our efforts to ensure the material prosperity of the country, we have not paid any attention to the spiritual element In human nature. Therefore, in order to give the individual and the nation a sense of purpose, something to live for, and If necessary to die for, we have to revive some philosophy of life and give a spiritual background to our thinking. We talk of welfare state and of democracy and of socialism, but they hardly convey a clear and unambiguous meaning. Democracy and socialism are means to an end and not an end in itself.

In our efforts to ensure the material prosperity of the country, we have not paid any attention to the spiritual element In human nature. Therefore, in order to give the individual and the nation a sense of purpose, something to live for, and If necessary to die for, we have to revive some philosophy of life and give a spiritual background to our thinking.

In considering these economic aspects of our problems, we have to keep in view the Vedantic ideals of life force which is the inner base of everything that exists."

THE INSTITUTIONAL FRAMEWORK

On this subject, a heated public debate has been going on in the west since 1848.

The Hindus have been always aware that Art is the product of the human mind, that human mind and social order constantly act and react upon each other, and that though, in the last analysis, human mind is a more decisive factor, the impact of social order on human mind is an indisputable fact.

The Hindus have been always aware that Art is the product of the human mind, that human mind and social order constantly act and react upon each other, and that though, in the last analysis, human mind is a more decisive factor, the impact of social order on human mind is an indisputable fact.

In any kind of creative work, the creator unites himself with the object of his creation. Excellence cannot be achieved unless and until the creator's 'I' merges itself completely with the object of his creation, the 'Non-I'. This is impossible for a Narcissus whose self-love does not allow him to identify himself completely with anything outside himself. The excellence in any creative work—be it Art, Literature or Science and Narcissism are incompatible with each other. Genuine and unreserved love for the object of creation is a must.

When Stalin declared that the basis of communism was hatred, Revered Sri Guruji remarked that the basis of Hinduness is Love. The significance of his remark in the context of creative activity was not then adequately appreciated.

Love being the indispensable source of all art, any social order not conducive to the generation, survival and growth of that precious, divine emotion cannot also be conducive to the flowering of Art.

In the recent times, this subject has been ably dealt with by Erich Fromm.

Love being the indispensable source of all art, any social order not conducive to the generation, survival and growth of that precious, divine emotion cannot also be conducive to the flowering of Art.

Like all humanists, Fromm also is against self-alienation, dehumanisation, thingification.

Industrial civilisation is guilty of all these sins.

In case of a carpenter, a goldsmith, a peasant or a painter, there is intimate personal relationship between the producer and his product. A modern factory worker has no such relationship with his product—all relationships are impersonal. For him, 'equality' means 'standardisation'. 'Equality' today means 'sameness', rather than 'oneness'. He is not an individual; he becomes a 'nine to fiver', a part of the labour force or the bureaucracy. All his activities are routinised and prefabricated. This loss of one's unique individuality was resented by Marx. "Assume," Marx said, "man as man, and his relation to the world as a human one, and you can exchange love only for love, confidence for confidence, etc. If you wish to enjoy art, you must be an artistically trained person.... Every one of your relationships to man and to nature must be a definite expression of your real, individual life corresponding to the object of your will." This is not feasible under modern industrialisation. The ultimate consequence of psychology should be love; but industrial psychology does not recognise this fact.

Fromm remarks, "If we speak about love in contemporary western culture, we mean to ask whether the social structure of western civilisation and the spirit resulting from it are conducive to the development of love. To raise the question is to answer it in the negative."

The principle underlying capitalistic society and the principle of love are incompatible... people capable of love, under the present system, are necessarily the exceptions; love is by necessity a marginal phenomenon in the present-day western society.

"The principle underlying capitalistic society and the principle of love are incompatible... people capable of love, under the present system, are necessarily the exceptions; love is by necessity a marginal phenomenon in the present-day western society. Not so much because many occupations would not permit of a loving attitude, but because the spirit of a production-centred, commodity-greedy society is such that only the non-conformist can defend himself successfully against it.... Important and radical changes in our social structure are necessary, if love is to become a social and not a highly individualistic, marginal phenomenon."

"If man is to be able to love, he must be put in his supreme place. The economic machine must serve him, rather than he serve it."

This is naturally the precondition for the growth of genuine Art also.

'Social Order' is a wide term; it encompasses the entire framework of socio-politico-economic institutions.

This is naturally the precondition for the growth of genuine Art also. 'Social Order' is a wide term; it encompasses the entire framework of socio-politico-economic institutions.

THE NATURE OF ART

The nature of art also has some bearing on the matter. Stating that in painting later Europe has done much and richly and with a prolonged and constantly renewed inspiration, but the Olympian gods of Phidias are qualitatively not on the same artistic level as the gods of Indian sculpture, such as Buddhas, Natarajas, the dances of Shiva. Aurobindo says that the difference arises from the different kind of mentality required by the arts, i.e., painting and sculpture.

The art of making in stone or bronze calls for a cast of mind which the ancients had and the moderns have not or have had only in rare individuals, an artistic mind not too rapidly mobile and self-indulgent, not too much mastered by its own personality and emotion and the touches that excite and pass, but founded rather on some great basis of assured thought and vision, stable in temperament, fixed in its imagination on things that are firm and enduring. The aesthetic self-indulgence which the soul of colour permits and even invites the attraction of the mobile play of life to which line of brush, pen or pencil gives latitude, are here forbidden or, if to some extent achieved, only within a line of restraint to cross which is perilous and soon fatal.

A later Europe has failed for the most part in sculpture, inspite of some great work by individuals, an Angelo or a Rodin, because it played externally with stone and bronze, took them as a medium for the representation of life and could not find a sufficient basis of profound vision or spiritual motive.

□

Part-III

THE DIRECTION

THE PARADOX

This is the traditional Hindu way of thinking with integralism as its basic character. Those ignorant or unmindful of this approach will not be able to evaluate properly the greatness of even western giants. Why was the philosopher Socrates inquisitive about the true nature of beauty and ugliness? When apparently unending controversy about the real import of the philosophies of Plato and Aristotle was ranging in Europe, the Artist Raphael resolved—for common European mind—the academic dispute by depicting Plato pointing to the heavens, and Aristotle pointing his hand most determindly at the ground beneath him, in course of his 'The School of Athens'.

In the West, there is a growing interest in, and appreciation for, such integralism, particularly after the Second World War in course of which the war-leaders found it expedient to adopt an inter-disciplinary approach. But dazzled by the glamour of the West, the Hindu intellectual, suffering from inferiority complex, is too willing to lose his identity; he opts for cultural self-alienation. (Recently, a tendency to revolt against such slavishness is also evident.)

Long back, Arnold Toynbee had observed: 'On the surface, those Hindus who have adopted one, to them, extremely alien Western culture on the planes of technology and science, language and literature, administration and law, appear to have been more successful than the Russians in harmonising with their native ways of life a Western way that is intrinsically more alien to them than it is to the Russians. Yet the tension in Hindu souls must be extreme, and, sooner or later, it must find some means of discharging itself."

According to Toynbee, the Western way of life is part and parcel of the Graeco Judiac heritage, and the whole of this cultural tradition is alien to the Hindu spirit. Therefore, sooner or later, the prodigal son's return will be inevitable. But in the meanwhile, the nation is being required to pay a very high price for the self-oblivion of these hypnotised Hindus. Unprecedented damage is being caused on account of this fact to every field of national life. The field of arts is no exception to this phenomenon.

According to Toynbee, the Western way of life is part and parcel of the Graeco Judiac heritage, and the whole of this cultural tradition is alien to the Hindu spirit. Therefore, sooner or later, the prodigal son's return will be inevitable.

CONFUSION OF CONCEPT

In the popular mind, there is no clear and comprehensive concept of art. The high-brow mentality which is the legacy of the western trend of compartmentalisation dominates the general thinking. For example, the art-galleries of the high-brows are reserved only for the glamorous arts of architecture, sculpture, painting, music, etc. No one knows what the place is of those genuine artists who are, for the sake of practical convenience, described as 'artisans' or 'craftsmen', in the total scheme of things. 'Vishvakarma' is the national deity of all creative labour. Can his 'sons' enter the sanctuary of Art?

Recently, the 'Dastakar' organised at Kochi the exhibition of traditional crafts. Around 40 traditional craftsmen from all over the country had descended on Kochi to exhibit their wares which gave a great surprise to the sophisticated art-lovers of Kerala. 'Patta' paintings from Orissa became articles of special attraction.

Recently, the 'Dastakar' organised at Kochi the exhibition of traditional crafts. Around 40 traditional craftsmen from all over the country had descended on Kochi to exhibit their wares which gave a great surprise to the sophisticated art-lovers of Kerala. 'Patta' paintings from Orissa became articles of special attraction. The Patta Painters based at Jagannath temple in Puri have a long tradition of 'sadhana', from generation to generation. Should they be excluded from the category of 'artists' simply because they are not sophisticated? Or because their varities of art are 'useful' but not 'fine'.

Any such 'avyapti' on purely technical or academic grounds damages the cause, not only of such sadhakas, but also of the whole country. That would mean depriving ourselves of the rich and glorious heritage of fine arts that have received sincere appreciation from foreigners also. See, for example, the following account of Will Durant:

Before Plassey, that is, in pre-British India, Durant says, "Every mature workman was a craftsman, giving form and personality to the product of his skill and taste. Even today, when factories replace handicrafts, and craftsmen degenerate into 'hands', the stalls and shops of every Hindu town show squatting artisans beating metal, moulding jewellery, drawing designs, weaving delicate shawls and embroideries, or carving ivory and wood. Probably, no other nation known to us has ever had so exuberant a variety of arts."

Any such 'avyapti' on purely technical or academic grounds damages the cause, not only of such sadhakas, but also of the whole country. That would mean depriving ourselves of the rich and glorious heritage of fine arts that have received sincere appreciation from foreigners also.

Durant further says: "If the vessel was to be made of some precious metal, then artistry could spend itself upon it without stint; witness the Tanjore silver vase in the Victoria Institute at Madras, or the gold Betel Dish of Kandy. Brass was hammered into an endless variety of lamps, bowls and containers; a black alloy (bidri) of zinc was often used for boxes, basins and trays; and one metal was inlaid or overlaid upon another, or encrusted with silver or gold. Wood was carved with a profusion of plant and animal forms. Ivory was cut into everything from deities to dice; doors and other objects of wood were inlaid with it; and dainty receptacles were made of it for cosmetics and perfumes. Jewellery abounded, and was worn by rich and poor as ornament or hoard; Jaipur excelled in firing enamel colours upon a gold background, clasps, beads, pendants, knives and combs were moulded into tasteful shapes, with floral, animal, or theological, designs; one Brahman pendant harbours in its tiny space half a hundred gods. Textiles were woven with an artistry never since excelled. From the days of Caesar to our own, the fabrics of India have been prized by all the world. Sometimes, by the subtlest and most painstaking of precalculated measurements, every thread of warp and woof was dyed before being placed upon the loom; the design appeared as the weaving progressed, and was identical on either side. From homespun Khaddar to complex brocades flaming with gold, from picturesque pyjamas to the invisibly seamed shawls of Kashmir, every garment woven in India has a beauty that comes only of a

Wood was carved with a profusion of plant and animal forms. Ivory was cut into everything from deities to dice; doors and other objects of wood were inlaid with it; and dainty receptacles were made of it for cosmetics and perfumes.

very ancient, and now almost instinctive, art."

Probably, the traditional jurisdiction of Art in our country was much wider. This is evident from the traditional enumeration of sixty-four arts.

It is wrong to presume that one particular art is superior to any other art. When asked by a devotee of music as to which art was superior to all others, Aurobindo replied, "You want me to give the crown or apple to Music and enrage the Goddesses of Painting, Sculpture, Architecture, Embroidery, all the Nine Muses? Your test of preference is wrong."

You want me to give the crown or apple to Music and enrage the Goddesses of Painting, Sculpture, Architecture, Embroidery, all the Nine Muses? Your test of preference is wrong.

"Each of the great arts has its own appeal and its own way of appeal and each in its own way is supreme above all others."

WHERE DO THEY STAND?

While it is true that in the sphere of arts, it is usually the inferior things that have the more general, if not quite universal, appeal, it is also a fact that in every country, there are bound to be different stages of regional or social development and different levels of artistic development corresponding to the former.

Take, for example, the case of 'Natyam'. Bharat Muni's 'Natya Shastra' is a complex work on Indian dramaturgy, a source book of all aspects of stagecraft, all aspects of dance, and the fundamentals of music. 'Natya' comprises all the three aspects.

The earliest cognisable roof of Indian music and dance is traceable in the Rig Veda. In Rig Veda, there is a mention of couples dancing in circles. Hymns in the form of dialogues, viz., the Sama Veda Sooktas with references to music and drama, are abundant in Vedic literature. The norms for music, dance and drama are given in the 'Vaajasanaayi Samhita' of the 'Shukla Yajur Veda.'

The earliest cognisable roof of Indian music and dance is traceable in the Rig Veda. In Rig Veda, there is a mention of couples dancing in circles. Hymns in the form of dialogues, viz., the Sama Veda Sooktas with references to music and drama, are abundant in Vedic literature.

No doubt, the Indian dance has travelled a long way since then. There is a prodigious wealth of literature on the glorious march of Indian Dance. The more important among the modern works are 'The Dance of Shiva' by Ananda Coomaraswamy, 'The Art of Dance' by Dr. C.P. Ramaswami Iyer, 'The Sacred Dance of India' by Mrinalini Sarabhai, 'Origin and Development of Thullal' by P.K. Sivasankara Pillai, 'Lesser Known Forms of Performing Arts in India' edited by Durgadas Mukhopadhyaya, 'Traditions of Indian Folk Dance' by Dr. Kapila Vatsayan, and 'Indian Dance As a Spiritual Art' by K.S. Ramaswami Sastri. This literature is an evidence of the tremendous progress registered by Indian Dance so far.

There have also been able exponents of this art in recent times.

Rukmini Devi who could reconstruct in dance a great life. Kuchipudi fame Yamini Krishnamoorthy, Shobha Naidu and Rani Kama of Andhra Pradesh. Bharatnatyam fame Dr. Padma Subramanian and Vyjayanti Mala of Tamil Nadu.

Along with Birju Maharaj, Udaya Shankar, the first Indian to present Indian ballet, a choreographer, who put India on the cultural map of the world and attempted to synthesise the different systems.

Vellathol of Kalamandalam who, brought to fruition the art of Koodiyatham dancers like Irinjalakkuda Madhavan Chakyar, and Kathakali dancers like Kalamandalam Krishnan Nair, Ramankutty Nair and Gopi; the virtuosity of Raja of Vellathunadu who refined Raja of Kottarakkara's Ramanattam—which in its turn was the successor of Manavedan Zamorin's Krishnanattam—to the finished form of Kathakali; and the aesthesis of the works of Bhasa, Kulashekhara, Varman, Sree Harsha, Mahendravikrama Pallava, Bodhayana, Shaktibhadra, Kattayam Raja, King Swati Tirunal, Unnayi Wariyar, and Irayimman Thampi.

Rukmini Devi who could reconstruct in dance a great life. Kuchipudi fame Yamini Krishnamoorthy, Shobha Naidu and Rani Kama of Andhra Pradesh.

Bharatnatyam fame Dr. Padma Subramanian and

Vyjayanti Mala of Tamil Nadu.

Mohiniyattam fame Kalyanikutti Amma.

In no way less prominent, other artists like Tara Choudari and Sitara Devi of Kathak, Darshana Jhaveri of Manipuri, Sonal Mansing of Odissi, and a host of other luminaries.

This is one, recognised, level of this art.

But that is not all.

As we are all aware, even more than the Western music, Western dance is becoming more popular today, particularly in the urban areas of northern parts. Every art has to suffer the lowering of standards brought about by unscrupulous charlatons and dabblers in the art. What is growing in influence today is not the more sophisticated variety of western dance like, say ballet or art of Anna Pavlova; what we witness more often is its cheap and, sometimes, vulgar variety. This should be a cause for great concern, because it has a direct and unhealthy impact on impressionable minds. These people are not interested in genuine art. They have no patience for Natyaveda or Natyashastra. They do not want to strain their nerves to bedome a Briju Maharaj or Udayashankara They are not

As we are all aware, even more than the Western music, Western dance is becoming more popular today, particularly in the urban areas of northern parts. Every art has to suffer the lowering of standards brought about by unscrupulous charlatons and dabblers in the art.

genuine lovers of art; they are 'arty' pretentiously claiming to be artistic.

Fortunately, this epidemic is confined to urban areas only.

As stated earlier, different levels of development within the same society during the same period is an important factor.

Recently, public leaders are paying more attention to scheduled tribes. It has come to their notice that our tribals in different regions have developed their own peculiar styles of dance and music. It would be simply impossible to enumerate the names of all these styles. Each tribe has its own styles and varieties of folk-dances of non-tribal, rural people. Both types of folk-dances. Then there are folk-dances usually portray the functions of daily life, rites and rituals, belief systems. They are performed on social occasions, such as, marriages, child-births, agricultural operations, changes in seasons, fairs festivals or religious ceremonies. All folk dances are accompanied by suitable music, such as light music used during Pigeon Dance, Kite Dance, Pot Dance, Plate Dance and Snake Dance. Each tribe has its own varieties. Gonds

Recently, public leaders are paying more attention to scheduled tribes. It has come to their notice that our tribals in different regions have developed their own peculiar styles of dance and music. It would be simply impossible to enumerate the names of all these styles.

have their ‘Jhumar’, ‘Saila’, ‘Rina’, and dances on ‘Karma’ festival and ‘Chaitra’ festival. Every province also has its own peculiar dances. For instance, in Rajasthan, we come across ‘Kachi Ghodi’, ‘Geeder’, the fire-dance of the Sidh Jats, ‘Tera Tali’ of the Kamar tribe, ‘Valar’ of the Garasias, ‘Dholi’, ‘Gauri’ and ‘Ghumar’ of Bhils, ‘Gher’ of the Mina tribe, ‘Raika’, ‘Jhoria’, etc. Some dances in different States have received more publicity, such as ‘Garba’ of Gujarat or ‘Bhangra’ of Punjab. But that does not mean that these States are not having other varities also. The street plays of Yakshagana’ of Karnataka and ‘Therukkoothu’ of Tamil Nadu are well-known. But other States also can boast of their own varieties of street plays.

But it is clearly evident that from the streets of the villages and mofussil towns to the majestic theatres of metropolitan cities equipped in the most modern western style, it is a very long leap. And between these two poles, there are a number of levels and stages.

On the whole, this is a very impressive spectrum, indeed.

But it is clearly evident that from the streets of the villages and mofussil towns to the majestic theatres of metropolitan cities equipped in the most modern western style, it is a very long leap. And between these two poles, there are a number of levels and stages.

The question is where will all those operating on this rustic level be placed by our high-brows, who are the recognised evaluators of this field? Our traditional criterion was different from that of these evaluators who are impressed by the glamour of pompous showmanship. Formerly, the sincere urge for, and the degree and intensity of, one's 'sadhana' determined whether one should be admitted to the prestigious class of 'artists'. Today, where will these genuine artists stand?

THE MOTIVATION

The greatest damage caused by westernisation to the sphere of Hindu Art has been on account of the drastic—or counter—revolutionary(?)—change in the motivation of artists, art lovers and art managers.

All Hindu Art orginates from, is dedicated to, and finds its fulfilment in, the realisation of the Absolute, the One without the second. This fact gives rise to its special characteristics. The following observation of Will Durant about Ajanta is representative of the general character of all Hindu arts. Durant says, "Here at Ajanta, religious devotion fused with architecture, sculpture and painting into a happy unity and produced one of the sovereign monuments of Hindu art." And, again, "Shiva himself was the god of dance and the dance of Shiva symbolised the very movement of the world. A commercially motivated dancer

Durant says, "Here at Ajanta, religious devotion fused with architecture, sculpture and painting into a happy unity and produced one of the sovereign monuments of Hindu art."

giving performance in a New York theatre will be surprised to learn that the 'natyam' of his predecessors—comprising a combination of dance, drama and music—was inspired by the motivation of attaining 'Moksha', the Supreme Bliss. The genuine artists of the past had no other goal in life except the single-minded life-long 'sadhana' of Art. A genuine artist is a channel and an instrument of something greater than his own artistic personality. He lives intensely and brings a world out of the combination of his inner and outer observation, vision, experience. Regarding intensity, it is worth noting that in his later days, Milton used to write fifty lines per day, and Virgil only nine. 'Savitri' was re-written twelve times. Adversities and challenges sharpen the edge of his intensity. We get the best out of Beethoven and Milton after the former became deaf and the latter blind. Meera burst out her most thrilling songs when she suffered worst from the pangs of separation. Under the dark shadow of death, John Bunyan completed his 'Pilgrim's Progress', Savarkar his 'Kamala', and Ramprasad Bismil his 'Sarfaroshi'. Such intensity only a genuine 'sadhaka' can possess. When questioned by a vain duchess as to how much time he had taken to complete his masterpiece, Leonardo da Vinci replied, "Sixty-one years, Madam." When told that

Regarding intensity, it is worth noting that in his later days, Milton used to write fifty lines per day, and Virgil only nine. 'Savitri' was re-written twelve times. Adversities and challenges sharpen the edge of his intensity.

each one of the changes he had introduced in his painting recently was a trifle, an irritated Michaelangelo said, "Each one of these changes may be a trifle, but all these trifles put together are not a trifle, it is something big."

Under ideal conditions, the artist and the art become one. "How can we know the dancer from the dance?" asks W.B. Yeats. Eliot goes further, "... and there is only the dance." This type alone can have legitimate claim to the honourable category of 'artists'. 'Sadhana' must be distinguished from commercialisation, genuine artists from traders in arts.

Under ideal conditions, the artist and the art become one. "How can we know the dancer from the dance?" asks W.B. Yeats. Eliot goes further, "... and there is only the dance." This type alone can have legitimate claim to the honourable category of 'artists'. 'Sadhana' must be distinguished from commercialisation, genuine artists from traders in arts.

Unfortunately, utilitarianism has come to dominate this field also.

There is a tendency to give too much importance to the commercial value of art, at the cost of its aesthetics. Enough financial resources to pay money for the stage, costumes, and the team of accompanying artistes; right contacts in the media to ensure publicity and image-building; access to official agencies meant for patronising artists,—all such factors are becoming more relevant than actual 'sadhana'. Very few are the students who strive to learn the basic elements and aspire to acquire knowledge of arts more for self-enlightenment and self-fulfilment. In the past, students underwent rigorous training from dedicated gurus. The art-institutes of today will find it difficult to survive if they follow the ideal of those gurus. And, again, such gurus are not in demand also, because every adolescent is in a great hurry to reach the radio or television.

Organisations for promoting arts are more concerned with the entertainment value. The listeners or the spectators are casual, and not earnest or suitably trained. Art lovers (virtuosos) have no necessary leisure or stamina to pursue cultivated appreciation.

Organisations for promoting arts are more concerned with the entertainment value. The listeners or the spectators are casual, and not earnest or suitably trained. Art lovers (virtuosos) have no necessary leisure or stamina to pursue cultivated appreciation. In this age of industrial civilisation, those engaged in arts are hedged for time, and art needs tranquility, composure and a reservoir of mental and physical energy. The temptation to yield to the lure of money and fame is too strong. Hence, the importance of advertising agencies. The art-managers are in a key-position; they can tactfully manipulate the artists and the art-lovers.

Consequently, commercial art is elbowing out genuine art. We are moving fast towards the disaster of mediocrity which, if not restrained immediately, will lead us to a catastrophe in the sphere of arts.

This apparently impossible task can be accomplished only through the restoration of the original spirit of Hinduness. This is the mission of 'Sanskar Bharati'. And for this purpose, it has to begin from the beginning.

When 'Sanskar Bharati' talks about Art, the westerners, or their camp-followers in our country, are bound to ask, what is the Sanskar Bharati's definition of 'Art'. On one occasion, Gurudev Rabindranath Tagore refused to define 'Art' before the western audience. Instead, he explained to them its function.

"Punashcha Harih Om"

What exactly is Art?

THE 'ART'

When 'Sanskar Bharati' talks about Art, the westerners, or their camp-followers in our country, are bound to ask, what is the Sanskar Bharati's definition of 'Art'.

On one occasion, Gurudev Rabindranath Tagore refused to define 'Art' before the western audience. Instead, he explained to them its function.

Did he feel that our concept of, and attitude towards, 'Art' would be beyond the comprehension of the westerners whose characteristic mental matrix is different from that of ours? He, however, took great pains to elaborate its functional aspect.

Discussions on "What is Art?" introduce elements of conscious purpose into the region where both our faculties of creation and enjoyment have been spontaneous and half-conscious. They aim at supplying us with every definite standards by which to guide our judgement of art productions. Therefore, we have heard judges in the modern time, giving verdict, according to some special rules of their own making, for the dethronement of immortals whose supremacy has been unchallenged for centuries.

Are creations of art to be judged either according to their fitness to be universally understood, or their philosophical interpretation of life, or their usefulness for solving the problems of the day, or their giving expression to something which is peculiar to the genius of the people to which the artist belongs?

Are creations of art to be judged either according to their fitness to be universally understood, or their philosophical interpretation of life, or their usefulness for solving the problems of the day, or their giving expression to something which is peculiar to the genius of the people to which the artist belongs?

Enjoyment is the soul of literature as well as of art. When analysed, its spectrum shows an endless series of rays of different colours and intensity throughout its different world of stars.

Man has a fund of emotional energy which is not all occupied with his self-preservation. This surplus seeks its outlet in the creation of Art, for man's civilisation is built upon his surplus.

In Art, man reveals himself and not his objects. His objects have their place in books of information and science, where he has completely to conceal himself.

> ***This world becomes completely our own when it comes within the range of our emotions. With our love and hatred, pleasure and pain, fear and wonder, continually working upon it, this world becomes a part of our personality.***
> ***It is not the fact of the sunrise, but its relation to ourselves, which is the object of perennial interest.***

The principal creative forces, which transmute things into our living structure, are emotional forces.

This world becomes completely our own when it comes within the range of our emotions. With our love and hatred, pleasure and pain, fear and wonder, continually working upon it, this world becomes a part of our personality.

It is not the fact of the sunrise, but its relation to ourselves, which is the object of perennial interest.

The things which arouse our emotions arouse our own self-feeling. What an artist has to say, he cannot express by merely informing and explaining. The plainest language is needed when I have to say what I know about a rose, but to say what I feel about a rose is different. There it has nothing to do with facts, or with laws; it deals with taste, which can be realised only by tasting.

In poetry, we have to use words which have got the proper taste—which do not merely talk, but conjure up pictures and sing. For pictures and songs are not merely facts, they are personal facts.

They are not only themselves, but ourselves also; they defy analysis and they have immediate access to our hearts.

When our heart is fully awakened in love, or in other great emotions, our personality is in its flood-tide. Then it feels the longing to express itself for the very sake of expression. Then comes Art, and we forget the claims of necessity, the thrift of usefulness,—the spires of our temples try to kiss the stars and the notes of our music to fathom the depth of the ineffable.

Man's energies, running on two parallel lines—that of utility and of self-expression—tend to meet and mingle.

Man's energies, running on two parallel lines—that of utility and of self-expression—tend to meet and mingle. In our life, we have one side which is finite, where we exhaust ourselves at every step, and we have another side, where our aspiration, enjoyment and sacrifice are infinite.

In our life, we have one side which is finite, where we exhaust ourselves at every step, and we have another side, where our aspiration, enjoyment and sacrifice are infinite.

This infinite side of man must have its revealments in some symbols which have the elements of immortality.

There it naturally seeks perfection.

This building of man's true world, the living world of truth and beauty, is the function of Art.

The truth has its enternal relation with the supreme person. Beauty is not a mere fact; it cannot be accounted for, it cannot be surveyed and mapped. It is an expression.

In these large tracts of nebulousness, Art is creating its stars—stars that are definite in their forms but infinite in their personality.

In Art, the person in us is sending its answers to the supreme person, who reveals himself to us in a world of endless beauty across the lightless world of facts.

In these large tracts of nebulousness, Art is creating its stars—stars that are definite in their forms but infinite in their personality.
In Art, the person in us is sending its answers to the supreme person, who reveals himself to us in a world of endless beauty across the lightless world of facts.

Probably, Gurudeva was right in apprehending the inherent incapacity of his audience in this particular matter.

As Rishi Aurobindo says:

The whole basis of Indian artistic creation is directly spiritual and intuitive, indicating infinite superiority of the method of direct perception over intellect.

Leonardo da Vinci's remarkable intuitions in science and his creative intuitions in art started from the same power, but the surrounding or subordinate mental operations were of a different character and colour. And in Art itself, there are different kinds of intuitions. (Intuitions of Shakespeare, Balzac or Ibsen)

The natural western mentality comes to Indian art with a damand for something other than what its characteristic spirit and motive intend to give, and, demanding that, is not prepared to enter into another kind of spiritual experience and another range of creative sight, imaginative power and mode of expression.

The natural western mentality comes to Indian art with a damand for something other than what its characteristic spirit and motive intend to give, and, demanding that, is not prepared to enter into another kind of spiritual experience and another range of creative sight, imaginative power and mode of expression.

All great artistic work proceeds from an act of intuition, not really an intellectual idea or a splendid imagination; these are only mental translations, but a direct intuition of some truth of life or being, some significant form of that truth, some development of it in the mind of man. And, so far, there is no difference between great European and great Indian work. Where then does the immense divergence begin? It is there in everything else, in the object and field of the intuitive vision, in the method or working out the sight or suggestion, in the part taken in the rendering by the external form and technique, in the whole way of the rendering to the human mind, even in the centre of our being to which the work appeals.

The theory of ancient Indian art at its greatest and the greatest gives its character to the rest and throws on it something of its stamp and influence—is of another kind. Its highest business is to disclose something of the self, the Infinite, the Divine to the regard of the soul, the Self through its expressions, the Infinite through its living finite symbols, the Divine through his powers. It is not that all Indian work realised this ideal; there is plenty, no doubt, that falls short, is lowered, ineffective or even debased, but it is the best and the most characteristic influence and execution which gives its tone to an art and by which we must judge. Indian art, in fact, is identical in its spiritual aim and principle with the rest of Indian culture. It is an intuititve and spiritual art and must be seen with the intuitive and spiritual eye.

The theory of ancient Indian art at its greatest and the greatest gives its character to the rest and throws on it something of its stamp and influence—is of another kind. Its highest business is to disclose something of the self, the Infinite, the Divine to the regard of the soul, the Self through its expressions, the Infinite through its living finite symbols, the Divine through his powers.

THE SCENE

The appreciation and evaluation of Hindu Arts and Hindu aesthesis by a Hindu can be considered as entirely subjective. The reaction of Margaret Noble, known to us as Sister Nivedita, to these subjects would be treated as more objective. A few of her observations on this topic would, therefore, be more appropriate and illuminating:

"Chitore is no mere chronological record, she is an eternal symbol, the heart's heart of one phase of the Indian genius."

"To all eternity, while the earth remains what she is, Ellora will be one of the spots where the mystery of God is borne in, in overwhelming measure, upon the souls of men, whatever their associations, whatever their creed."

"Like the curves and columns of some great organ, runs the line of stone arches and colonnades along the hillside that faces to the sunrise, in the glen of Ajanta."

"To all eternity, while the earth remains what she is, Ellora will be one of the spots where the mystery of God is borne in, in overwhelming measure, upon the souls of men, whatever their associations, whatever their creed."

"In all lands, the monk has memorialised himself by buildings instead of by posterity. In India, these have been largely carved, as at Mahabalipuram in the South, or excavated, as at Ellora and elsewhere, instead of built. But the sentiment is the same."

"Here in these lovely retreats—for they are all placed

in the midst of natural beauty—was elaborated the thought and learning, the power of quiet contemplation, that have made India as we know her today. Here were dreamt those dreams, which, reflected in society, became the social ideals of the ages in which we live."

> ***Beauty of place translates itself to the Indian consciousness as God's cry to the soul. Had Niagara been situated on the Ganges, it is odd to think how different would have been its valuation by humanity. Instead of fashionable picnics and railway pleasure-trips, the yearly or monthly incursion of worshipping crowds.***

"It is certain that behind sanctity of pilgrimage lies admiration of place, of art, even of geographical significance."

"Beauty of place translates itself to the Indian consciousness as God's cry to the soul. Had Niagara been situated on the Ganges, it is odd to think how different would have been its valuation by humanity. Instead of fashionable picnics and railway pleasure-trips, the yearly or monthly incursion of worshipping crowds. Instead of hotels, temples. Instead of ostentatious excess, austerity. Instead of the desire to harness its mighty forces to the chariot of human utility, the unrestrainable longing to throw away the body, and realise at once the ecstatic madness of Supreme Union."

"High among the Western Himalayas, close to the borders of Ladakh, lies the long glacial gorge in which is the famous cave of Amarnath. The awesome grandeur and beauty of the heights about them will always be remembered by them (pilgrims) as the great God's fit dwelling place. They are in a church. Rocks and glaciers form the sanctuary. Snow passes are the pillared aisels. Behind them stand the pine forests for processions of singers carrying banners, and overhead are the heavens themselves for cathedral roof. It is the peculiarity of Eastern people to throw upon the whole of Nature that feeling which we associate only with the place of worship."

TO THE ARTISTS

"Hinduism, in one of its aspects, is neither more nor less than a great school of symbolism. The appeal of this symbolism, moreover, is universal. It matters not what be the language spoken, nor whether the reader be literate or illiterate, the picture tells its own story, and tells it unmistakably:"

"Hinduism, in one of its aspects, is neither more nor less than a great school of symbolism. The appeal of this symbolism, moreover, is universal. It matters not what be the language spoken, nor whether the reader be literate or illiterate, the picture tells its own story, and tells it unmistakably:"

"An Indian painting, if it is to be really Indian and really great, must appeal to the Indian heart in an Indian way, must convey some feeling or idea that is either familiar or immediately comprehensible; and must further, to be of the very highest mark, arouse in the spectator a certain sense of a revelation for which he is the nobler."

"Art must be reborn. Not the miserable travesty of would be Europeanism that we at present know, there is no voice like that of art to reach the people. A song, a picture, may be the fiery cross that reaches all the tribes, and makes them one. And art will be reborn, for she has found a new subject—India herself."

"Art must be reborn. Not the miserable travesty of would be Europeanism that we at present know, there is no voice like that of art to reach the people. A song, a picture, may be the fiery cross that reaches all the tribes, and makes them one. And art will be reborn, for she has found a new subject—India herself."

"The man who has not entered into the whole culture of his epoch can hardly create a supreme expression of that culture."

"Art, then, is charged with a spiritual message—in India today, the message of the Nationality."

"Let two men take up the study of art in the right spirit, and they will change the whole art world of India."

"Hence, art offers us the opportunity of a great common speech, and its rebirth is essential to the up-building of the motherland—its reawakening rather."

"For art, like science, like education, like industry, like trade itself, must now be followed "For the re-making of the Motherland"—and for no other aim."

THE WAY

'Sanskar Bharati' is born to facilitate the Hindu Art to play its role as thus envisaged by Sister Nivedita. She also knew that the Hindu goal of individual life is 'Atmano Mokshartham-Jagad Hitayacha', that, is, 'Salvation of the self and welfare of the world.' It implies that the natural corollary of Hindu Renaissance is Human Renaissance—though it would have been too premature during her life-time to proclaim so. Stating that "in India there is an attitude towards life and an approach to the handling of human affairs, that answers to the needs of the world as a whole." Arnold Toynbee exhorts, "If India were ever to fail to live up to this Indian ideal which is the finest, and, therefore, the most exacting legacy in your Indian heritage, it would be a poor look out for mankind as a whole. So, a great spiritual responsibility rests on India."

'Sanskar Bharati' is born to facilitate the Hindu Art to play its role as thus envisaged by Sister Nivedita. She also knew that the Hindu goal of individual life is 'Atmano Mokshartham-Jagad Hitayacha', that, is, 'Salvation of the self and welfare of the world.' It implies that the natural corollary of Hindu Renaissance is Human Renaissance—though it would have been too premature during her life-time to proclaim so.

Maladies of the human society are many; and many are

the remedies tried for them so far. But none of them seems to have touched the root of the problem. In 'Evolution and the Earthly Destiny', Nolini Kanta Gupta remarks:

"We badly needed a United National Organisation, but we are facing the utmost possible disunity. The lesson is that politics alone will not save us, nor even economics. The word has gone forth; what is required is a change of heart. The leaders of humanity must have a new heart grafted in place of old."

Cousin's line of thinking would remind one of a remark by Revered Dr. Hedgewar. He said, "In our country, there are so many colleges of arts, but there are no colleges of heart." The tortured mind of humanity can find a new ray of hope in Cousin's assertion. Arts, according to him, can have sobering effect on even criminals and terrorists.

But is such a 'change of heart' feasible?

"Yes", says a sane but feeble voice.

There still remains one remedy that has not yet been given a trial for this purpose.

What is it?

Aesthesis.

After the end of the Second World War, an effort for the construction of new human society was initiated. The economic, the political and the religious freedoms are valuable for this purpose. But will they be adequate, in absence of the aesthetic sense? This question has been posed by J.H. Cousins in his 'The Aesthetic Necessity of Life'. The author asserts that without restraining human passions through aesthetic sense, new society cannot be evolved. Intelligence without human heart can be dangerous.

Cousin's line of thinking would remind one of a remark by Revered Dr. Hedgewar. He said, "In our country, there are so many colleges of arts, but there are no colleges of heart."

The tortured mind of humanity can find a new ray of hope in Cousin's assertion. Arts, according to him, can have sobering effect on even criminals and terrorists.

This seems to be an indispensable supplementary measure for the purpose.

In that case, organisations like 'Sanskar Bharati' are sure to be called upon to play a significant role on the international plane also.

> ***Arnold Toynbee had said, "Today we are still living in this transitional chapter of the world's history, but it is already becoming clear that a chapter which had a Western beginning will have to have an Indian ending if it is not to end in the self-destruction of the human race.... At this supremely dangerous moment in human history, the only way of salvation for mankind is an Indian way."***

Arnold Toynbee had said, "Today we are still living in this transitional chapter of the world's history, but it is already becoming clear that a chapter which had a Western beginning will have to have an Indian ending if it is not to end in the self-destruction of the human race.... At this supremely dangerous moment in human history, the only way of salvation for mankind is an Indian way."

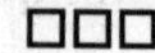